THE
Intuitive C
Finding Creative Freed ...arden

TEXT & PHOTOGRAPHS BY MARILYN RAFF

Fulcrum Publishing
Golden, Colorado

To my husband, Jeff,

for his constant love and support

❦

and to my friend Waynelle Wilder

for opening the door

Library of Congress Cataloging-in-Publication Data

Raff, Marilyn.
   The intuitive gardener : finding creative freedom in the garden /
text and photographs by Marilyn Raff.
      p. cm.
Includes bibliographical references (p.   ).
   ISBN 1-55591-442-X (pbk. : alk. paper)
   1. Landscape gardening—West (U.S.) 2. Landscape gardening. I.
Title.
SB470.54.W3 R34 2002
712'.6'0978—dc21
                    2002004226

Printed in China
0 9 8 7 6 5 4 3 2 1

Editorial: Marlene Blessing, Alice Copp Smith, Daniel Forrest-Bank
Design: Constance Bollen, cb graphics
Cover image: *Papaver dubium* (long-headed poppy) bends in the summer sun.
Copyright © Marilyn Raff.

Fulcrum Publishing
16100 Table Mountain Parkway, Suite 300
Golden, Colorado 80403
(800) 992-2908 • (303) 277-1623
www.fulcrum-books.com

Contents

Rosa x *harisonii* (Harison's yellow rose) acts as a billowing backdrop against solid granite rock.
On the far left, the peachy blooms of *Papaver triniifolium* (Armenian poppy), with touches of steely blue
Picea pungens 'Glauca Procumbens' (bottom left), are balanced against a sea of shocking pink Dianthus.
Rounding out the panorama in the right foreground is *Aurinia saxatilis* (basket-of-gold).

Introduction

❧

At midlife my future began to crystallize. The kids were almost grown and gone, or at least moving along on their paths. I was on a mission to discover my destiny. *Flashdance* was on the big screen, and I vividly recall wondering when and how I would find my passion. What was my myth?

Fifteen years earlier and newly married, my husband and I had moved to Zurich, Switzerland, to study at the Jung Institute there. I attended many classes on dreams, various aspects of personal growth, and alchemy. I learned that during the Middle Ages the alchemists were concerned with transformation. As the earliest chemists, they focused, in their laboratories, not only on attempting to change base metals into gold, but also on the spiritual work of soul transformation. In his work Dr. Carl Jung amplified this aspect of the alchemists' theme—the transformation of our inner souls. For five years, during my own process of analysis, I continually heard terms such as "vessel," "transformation," and "change." I was fascinated with unearthing the past and seeking to heal old wounds. The metaphor of transformation had tremendous resonance for me. It became the lens through which I viewed the world, and led me to what was to become my life's work—gardening: a continual process of creating, re-creating, and transforming natural elements.

As I describe the evolution of building my little piece of paradise, I am hopeful that other gardeners will be encouraged to create their own Garden of Eden. This process combines taking the pulse of the garden with being in tune with our inner senses. Just as tradesmen and

Above: Wide-open
Tulipa kaufmanniana 'Ancilla'.

artists have their tricks of the trade, the trick for intuitive gardeners is to discover and follow their own internal feelings of what is "right" in their gardens. By following these innermost hunches over time, they will experience what "looks and feels right" to them. As this sense is nurtured, practiced, and developed, they will see more triumphs. Of course, as in any facet of life, there will be blunders and all sorts of adventures. Yet, the intuitive gardener will learn that to garden is to be flexible; there are no strict rules, only guidelines that you create. If mistakes happen—and they certainly will—practically anything can be changed or moved, depending on your wishes and impulses. This permissive approach to gardening, unencumbered by the opinions of experts, is refreshing and uninhibited. It opens up the door to unknown pleasures as gardeners tap into these feelings that are often just beneath the surface in their psyches.

After my return to the United States from Zurich, I focused on "inside" or internal affairs—my family and my personal growth—for years. Our children were raised discussing dreams at the breakfast table. But as they grew I began to look around "outside" for a fulfilling and meaningful way to be in the world. I longed to discover my passion. While I was completing my education, I wondered about a career as a therapist, assisting others in their searches. But that was too sedentary a job for me. I needed something more physical and closer to my heart.

Then it happened. On a whim I wandered into the Denver Botanic Gardens. For years I had been the kind of gardener who poked a few petunias into the ground. I thought perhaps I could volunteer there, since someone always needs help at these large establishments. Although a complete novice, I had heard the term "rock gardening," so I inquired about the topic. "Go see Panayoti," I was told nonchalantly by a knowledgeable-looking staff member with impressive tools strapped to his belt. "He can help you." What an unusual name, I thought to myself, and it piqued my interest.

I strolled at a casual pace to what seemed to be the outskirts of the garden, barely glancing at the plants along the edges of the wide, squared-off paths. There I met Panayoti Kelaidis, at the time Curator of the Denver Botanic Gardens Rock Alpine Garden, a friendly gentleman who heartily welcomed me into his garden family and unpretentiously explained what he and his crew did: "We weed, plant, move plants, dig, amend soil, and maintain this garden." I reflected for a moment. This physical activity sounded reasonably fun. Yes, I was ready to dig in and help in any way that I could.

As if attending a ritual, once a week for many years, regardless of weather conditions, I went to the Rock Alpine Garden to volunteer my services. Along with a handful of others, I worked, weeded, and chatted. Some mornings we planted, and other times we shoveled soil, raked the crushed granite paths smooth, or spruced up a section of the garden. Panayoti always had a list of chores. I was pleased to be able to pick and choose the tasks that attracted me.

Planting was the most fun. I learned about spacing plants correctly and the importance of making sure the plant was placed securely in the ground. I pressed my fingers around the crown of the plant and pushed down gently but firmly so that the plant wouldn't heave, or pop out, during inclement weather or any other time throughout the year. Typical of a large botanic garden, or any garden, was the routine of weeding. There was much of it to be done, and I did it often. The job had two important aspects: having the right equipment or tools and—critical to the process—knowing a weed from a desirable plant! The morning sessions lasted four or five hours. Then we'd stay for lunch, often listening to Panayoti wax poetic about plants and people, his favorite topics. Because we were volunteers, Panayoti gave us a few extra plants now and then.

My passion started slowly, like a locomotive chugging along, but it gathered speed dramatically each month. If a particular plant intrigued me, I would head over to the Gardens' library to research it. I unraveled the path of *Papaver triniifolium*, one of my favorite poppies. Long ago plant explorers tracked it to the hills of Asia Minor. From there, it made its way to the botanic garden in Göteborg, Sweden. According to well-kept records at the Denver Botanic Gardens, the Göteborg Botanical Garden is where Panayoti first obtained seed twenty years ago.

I also took a class on soils through the Colorado Federation of Garden Clubs. As the instructor talked about composting and soil composition, I had a flash of recognition: "This sounds like alchemy to me, but with different ingredients."

For gardeners, soil is the all-important *prima materia*—the material to be transformed. Compost, itself a product of transformation, is a magical ingredient. Aside from aerating compacted clay or binding the loose particles in sand, it creates rich and friable soil that is worth its weight in gold. My neighbors grew accustomed to seeing some form of compost piled high in my driveway. Usually, within a few days the piles dwindled down as I shoveled and hauled this precious material, spreading it over my beds as a topdressing.

Yet gardening is not only about planting, digging, and hauling; that's just the labor end and the start of this creative process. It's mainly about the beauty we are creating. A distinctive behavior of the passionate gardener, which usually occurs in the early morning but can happen spontaneously at any time of day, is a leisurely walk through her creation, without tools or weeding gear, but perhaps with a cup of coffee in hand. I often walk out to my garden this way, to gaze at an intricate bloom or an inspired floral grouping.

In this book, I've tried to amplify the process of creating such billowing plant compositions and to show that there are unlimited possibilities in the garden once distinctive elements— rocks, paths, flowers—are put together with imagination and intuition.

Shimmering silver *Chrysothamnus nauseosus* (rabbitbrush) in the background accentuates the velvety *Papaver somniferum* 'Lauren's Grape' (poppy).

Photograph By Donna Demeter

CHAPTER ONE

Intuitive Imagination

❧

Two forces propel me to garden: imagination and intuition. It is through these two faculties that I am able to develop all my different gardens. Through intuition I see possibilities—I know what to plant in a particular site. When my imagination kicks in, it forms images that fill the empty canvas that is my backyard. Sometimes an idea comes quickly. At other times it evolves over days, weeks, or even months, because for some sites much inward psychic "cooking" is needed in order for ideas to become concrete. I have never drawn a design nor measured a border. That approach appeals to others, but it is not my way. It would take away my fun

Above: Flowershop sign
in Santa Fe, New Mexico.

My ratty and boring backyard in Littleton, Colorado, 1985.

and excitement and the challenge of discovery. Working at my desk for hours or measuring areas outdoors requires too much attention to detail and tedious thinking.

I am a hands-on person. In fact, when I am designing a border or figuring out a plan, I use my hands, arms, and feet frequently. Colleagues laugh as I crazily move my arms about, imagining the length of a border or deciding how many plants will fit into it. Moving about stimulates my imagination. I might walk through my garden to estimate how many plants I need to complete a floral scene, and I may make a few notes — but only if the spirit moves me.

I totally trust my intuition to tell me what will satisfy my senses in terms of design elements and plant choices. For instance, in one sunny area along a fence, I felt that something with height was necessary. I imagined how a thirty-foot tree would look in that spot; then I immediately purchased and planted one that would grow to that size. Years later, I am still pleased with my choice.

I believe that many gardeners use this intuitive approach. They think, "I want to make my garden look pretty…this colorful plant is pretty…I'll buy this plant." Or "My neighbor has a clematis…I want one too." Or "My fall garden is drab. I'll swing by the nursery on my way home from work and see if there is a plant that can zip it up. While I'm there, I might pick up a few bulbs to bring me out of the winter doldrums next spring." These are intuitive pursuits: *a process of direct knowing without the conscious use of reasoning.* One idea or thought jumps into another.

Even when I had gardening clients, my best tools were my eyes and my intuition. After a few minutes (or maybe a few days), I could "draw" the design mentally. I would shuffle ideas within myself and ask such questions as "Do I want a mound here, or something statuesque? Would a curved border be right for this bed? Should a rock go here? Where could I use strong color or texture most appropriately?" My intuition worked overtime until I made some decisions, eliminating choices that did not fit into my scheme. My only physical tool would be a simple garden hose, which became the outline of borders and gave me a rough sense of their sizes.

Books and catalogs bring together ideas for me. I read them most frequently in winter and enjoy their mouth-watering descriptions, written to entice gardeners to buy for the upcoming season. I don't give much thought as to where any of this new inventory is going to be planted, or even whether there is room! So I may check off many items one week, then add or eliminate some the following week. Reality sets in only when my orders arrive in spring and I need to imagine where these newly acquired gems can be planted.

My intuitive way of doing things really goes bonkers when I shop locally for plants. As I wheel my cart to different sections of the nursery, from perennials to grasses to shrubs, I buy whatever appeals to me. Yes, I do act impulsively. But this is my passion, and I give myself permission to enjoy myself to the max. There are many "must-have"s. I pay particular attention to new introductions or to plant names that spark my curiosity.

On occasion, before leaving home, I may jot down a few notes about specific items that I want—but only if I feel like it. When I arrive at the nursery or garden center I'll check with employees about those plants I've listed. I'm thrilled if they're in stock, but I'll also check out all the rows of plants neatly arranged on the ground. Sometimes an employee or an owner is excited about what he is selling, and his enthusiastic and detailed plant description sets my intuition off and running. I often buy more than I had planned.

Real enjoyment comes when I arrive home and, tenderly holding the plants in my hands, look for the perfect place to plant them. I usually have an assortment of plant sizes, everything from two-inch pots all the way up to five-gallon ones. With trowel or shovel in hand, I begin the roaming process. As I linger in different areas in search of cozy spots, I briefly think about each plant's needs. Does it desire sun or shade, a moist or a dry site? Will it sprawl or crawl, grow large or stay small? All these ideas and more come into play as I imagine where the plant will look best. But my main criterion is my intuition. It tells me how well the new arrival will harmonize with surrounding plants and structures.

Burgundy fall color of *Euphorbia palustris* (spurge) in front of the glowing leafage of *Betula occidentalis* (western river birch).

Some days I don't find the right home for the plant, so I put it off to the side and keep it adequately watered. I'll wait for a few days or weeks, until I imagine a place where it will fit. In the meantime, maybe I'll clean up an area or move other plants to give me openings for new individuals. Or, as I stroll my garden again, I might notice a spot that I missed in the first go-around. I may intuitively know then that my new plant belongs there. And I may dream how it will bind its companions together when it grows to maturity. So I continually play back and forth from imagination to intuition, from intuition to imagination, to build, refine, and transform my garden from a simple group of plants into a cohesive ensemble.

A Garden Evolves

My garden has evolved gradually since the mid-1980s. Whenever I had a sparkling idea I tried to implement it. Because drawing my ideas on paper didn't work for me, I had to imagine the plan. Then I could slowly flesh it out as I worked and change it as necessary. For me, as for many others, gardening is not a rational process; its logic is of a different order, connected to heart and intuition. I am driven by an inner urge to create brilliance out of raw elements.

My first sparkling idea, back in 1979, was a rather bland one: to put down grass around my newly constructed home. Boring, yes, but I was not a gardener at that time and was not remotely familiar with flowering plants. I'm from New Jersey, and I "knew" that grass had to go into every bare spot. That's what I saw practically everywhere in my suburban neighborhood. So, with my husband and some friends, I laid sod all over my east-facing front yard and in portions of my backyard. (My entire landscape is about half an acre and pie-shaped, fanning out from front to back, with three-quarters of this wedge in the backyard.) I was delighted to have something on the ground—anything rather than bare dirt!

During the sod-laying frenzy, a kind friend dropped by and gave us a multistemmed cottonwood tree. Not having any idea of its growth habit or the conditions it required, I planted it instantly in the center of the front yard. I was thrilled again, now that I had something other than grass to look at.

After a few years this scene became dull: grass and a tree. I wanted color! I browsed the nurseries and learned that in a shady site annual impatiens would work. A knowledgeable employee at the nursery told me I needed to remove some grass around my tree, then add compost and dig it in. I purchased a few bags of compost and followed his instructions. Every spring during those early gardening years, this was my routine—and the total extent of my front garden. I was a novice, exploring uncharted territory, happy to view a sea of impatiens that bloomed from May to September.

But soon I wanted even more color! I grew tired of seeing only impatiens. Once again, out came grass along my driveway and in went a narrow, three-foot border of petunias. That idea lasted for a few years. Then my intuition acted up yet again, and I felt that I needed something more substantial in this front area.

"What about a fence of some kind?" I thought to myself. "That might add some oomph." I planned on planting a border in front of a split-rail fence, which would separate my property from the adjacent street and sidewalk. I liked the idea of using wood in the garden because of its natural appearance, even though it breaks down more quickly than other, more durable materials. A wooden fence might need repair occasionally and would probably warrant replacement after twenty years. But I figured that after that much time I might be ready for a new design scheme anyhow!

To mimic the straight lines of the fence and on the advice of a garden center employee, I randomly bought tall plants such as digitalis (foxglove) and aconitum (monkshood). The fence also supports clematis vines and various other plants that lean against it and wander through and around it.

As I began building this garden, a few thoughts began to simmer. It was at about this time that, wanting to learn more about plants, I had begun to volunteer at the Denver Botanic Gardens. I also realized that carrying soil in by the bagful was a major pain (not to mention expensive), so I bought a small used truck to haul in soil by the cubic yard, as well as to transport other materials such as plants and fencing.

I dug out the grass along my new fence and wheelbarrowed it to my backyard, knowing that I could use it in some way later. Since I didn't want to get rid of all the grass, I pulled out my garden hose to help me decide how wide a border I desired and what kind of line was needed to separate the grass from the garden. Over the years I've learned that my hose is a handy design aid to my intuition: I lay it out to make a border that is aesthetically pleasing to my eyes. My instincts told me that curves would help soften the hard, straight lines of my rectangular house and the square angles of both the driveway and the front sidewalk.

I began with a mere three-foot-wide border and hauled in compost for it with my newly purchased truck. I spread this compost quite thickly (three to four inches) but evenly over the bed and dug it in. I was learning from my volunteer work that digging amendments down to a depth of eight or twelve inches would help to mix these ingredients with my clay soil, aerating it so that the roots of the plants could travel easily through the soil, providing a better environment for roots. Clay soils tend to be extremely compact and tight, limiting the amount of air and oxygen that plants need to grow successfully. Sandy soil needs amendments also, so that water will not drain quickly, leaching out valuable nutrients. Amendments for both soil types are an important energy source for bacteria, fungi, and earthworms that live in the soil. (I am well aware that many plants native to a particular region do not necessarily need the addition of organic matter to produce flowers and remain healthy. Because I mix a wide assortment of plants together, I trust my intuition to tell me what quantity of amendments I'll need and how rich the soil should be in any particular bed.)

As my experience increased and as the seasons rolled on, I stretched my borders. The three-foot border over time became six feet wide, and the skinny border around the fast-growing cottonwood tree kept getting wider as well. I needed to widen the borders because I was accumulating more knowledge and confidence about plants and thus I could install more of them. The inner excitement of learning about plants and buying more of them increased daily. I even purchased a special, extra-sharp edging tool to make grass removal easier. My technique was simple: I sprayed weed killer, waited for the grass to die, and then turned it over and added a few inches of compost on top. At other times, I didn't bother spraying but just removed the grass, anxious to plant as quickly as possible.

Depending on my mood at the moment, I did whatever I felt like doing.

I began to experiment with perennials. (I had learned that perennials are plants that come back each year, not needing to be replanted as annuals do.) I cut down on the number of impatiens I bought, but I still found pleasure in planting a few on a curve in front of the perennials, where their bright coral and pink shades enhanced the entire garden. Even now I stretch the bed around my cottonwood each year (it's now an impressive twenty feet in diameter), further reducing the amount of grass in this area. Neither my husband nor I are fond of mowing lawn, so we are both happy when there is less of it.

I also removed more grass in order to soften the entryway to my house. To echo my maturing cottonwood, I imagined a walkway of thick wooden circles, cut from old tree stumps. I wanted to lay them in a random pattern and "plant" them in the dirt. I bought these slices and then prepared them with a black, water-resistant coating so that they would last for many years. And only recently, after fifteen years, did they start to deteriorate. I've replaced them with round concrete circles, patterned to mimic wood. In the midst of this forestlike, semi-shaded environment I have planted groundcovers and low perennials, mostly from two-inch containers so that they'll fit easily into the small spaces (two to six inches) that I left between the rounds. Plants in shades of silver, chocolate-leafed plants, and others of intricate texture draw your eyes to the ground, spotlighting the path. I planted some with care, but for the most part, I planted them by chance; wherever I thought they would look best I dug a hole and stuffed them in. As my garden has grown and reseeded itself, I've let a few volunteers spring up here and there to create a wider variety of textures.

The Tree

My cottonwood tree is not a choice specimen, but I hesitate to eliminate it now because it is huge and provides necessary shade. Fall cleanup is a major chore as its waxy leaves clutter the perennials beneath. I was not a perceptive plantswoman those many years ago—had I been, I would not have planted a cottonwood at all, and especially not twenty feet from my front door! However, now that it has reached maturity, I am pleased with this tree. Its five trunks, each over a foot thick, add remarkable weight, structure, and background effect, anchoring the potpourri of perennials that dwell beneath its branches.

I scoff at the conventional wisdom that says very little can grow beneath the canopy of a cottonwood because of its shallow root system. As I discovered, large shrubs are not pleased with this location, because they have to compete for water and nutrients. Yet hundreds of perennials, ornamental grasses, bulbs, and annuals grow vigorously here and are overjoyed

Reddish leaves of *Aronia melanocarpa* (black chokeberry) mingle among the sandy colors of autumn.

to call this habitat home. To help continue their success, I routinely add soil, but I am careful not to add so much as to interfere with the vitality and health of the cottonwood. This garden is lush and diverse through most of the growing season and has strong visual impact in spring and summer. With some shrubs anchoring the edge of this border and a few dwarf evergreens appropriately placed near the center, there is winter interest as well.

To balance the tree's heaviness and thickness, several three-foot grasses, with their fine texture, sway in the breeze during autumn and display tassel-like flowers at their tips in summer. Making good use of the tree is *Euonymus fortunei* 'Coloratus' (purpleleaf winter creeper). This broad-leaved evergreen groundcover, with dark green foliage in summer, turns purple-red in winter. It will crawl around the edge of the corky-barked trunks of the cottonwood and, without any other support, creep up them a few feet.

Framing the Outskirts

About ten feet out from the south side of my house I built a low berm, about two feet high, to make a long, narrow rock garden. Good-sized shrubs stand like soldiers at each end, adding structure and variety to the smooth, windowless wall of the house. Perched in the center of this rocky berm is a large *Ephedra equisetina* (horsetail joint fir). The narrow blue-green foliage is attractive next to the blank, peach-colored wall. (More about this plant in Chapter Two.) At the foot of this texture-laden shrub is a generous bed of various-sized drought-tolerant plants. In this hot and dry location, I water very little, and there is minimal maintenance.

If you approach my backyard garden, which is my biggest, you'll be faced with what appears to be a continuous sea of flowers. However, upon closer examination, and as you begin to wander from one garden room to the next, you'll see that each area is framed or set off from the next in some way—by a fence, various plant materials, edges, or paths.

My major frame is a solid-wood privacy fence. It surrounds most of my backyard and is the back border of both my garden and my property. This hardscape material defines the garden space and contains and displays the qualities within. Frames, no matter the material, give a sense of enclosure and set some kind of boundary. They also add structure, and they should contribute to the visual aesthetic of the overall garden scene.

When a plant material is used to create a boundary, it has a different effect from that of wood or stone or some other hardscape material. Its framing effect also depends on whether the plant material is evergreen or if it is a deciduous tree. Both will add softness, structure, and density, but each offers something different. The evergreen will be just that, green all year round, but it may need special care such as shearing to keep it in shape and away from the perennials. Deciduous trees or shrubs, once mature, make good boundaries, but when the leaves fall, there is more exposure. Their branches and trunks can be attractive even without leaves, but the sense of privacy will not be as strong as it is with the more structural evergreens. When choosing a framing plant, consider the eventual size and shape of the tree or shrub. Will it stay compact, or will it envelop the garden? Time and patience are needed for any living framework to mature, while a fence or a wall gives immediate results.

Consider your requirements. Do you need to keep kids and pets in? Or perhaps keep wild animals out? Will plant material work as well as a built structure? Do you desire a more spacious and open garden look (which plants will give), as opposed to the closed-in feeling of a metal or wooden fence? How close together should you plant? How dense a screen do you want? How much care do you want to invest in the outer edge of your garden? I encourage fellow gardeners to consider their particular needs. Think about your individual lifestyle and what will be ideal for your situation. Call on an outside landscape design expert, or stay with your own spontaneous ideas.

Fences not only serve as frames; they are great materials to grow plants on or near. Shrubs or trees in front of a fence add another layer of intrigue and more bulk to the garden. In one of my far corners where the fence turns, I have planted an *Acer grandidentatum* (big-tooth maple). This slow-growing large shrub or small tree, a Rocky Mountain native, is conical in shape and will eventually reach a height of thirty to forty feet, adding verticality and structure to this back niche. The ground slopes down toward this corner, so the plant gets the moisture it needs. In fall, as I sit on my patio many feet away, I can watch its green foliage turn fiery shades of orange and red.

Along this same fence I have added turkey wire, secured with strong staples, so that a few of my shrub roses can climb it. I recently planted the vigorous species rose *Rosa canina* (dog rose), which the fence now supports. This pinkish white, fragrant, single rose may grow five to ten feet high; in fall it has globular red hips.

The large unfenced openings on either side of my house are significant, too. These passageways are like spacious open doors; they invite you to stroll through my garden. They've

---

TIPS FOR GARDENERS

• If your garden has many straight lines, imagine what curves you can insert to soften the edges. If the edges are abundantly curved, add a few straight lines for variety.

• When shopping at a nursery, look for plants that will contrast with your already existing array of plants. Give yourself permission to buy when the desire is strong. Buy what excites you and stumbles across your path. See what colors, shapes, and textures seduce you.

• If you are bored with the same old plants year after year, experiment and try something different. Diversify and expand.

• Take time to slowly stroll through and carefully examine your garden. Jot down notes or not. Look for spots where a new plant or structure of some kind might enliven the area.

• If you've been planning to install a new flower bed and have been stalling, get started—don't wait until you've planned every little detail. As you begin the project, ideas will bubble up about bed size and your choice of plants. Adjustments can be made later.

• Be radical and defiant. Use a plant or reach for an idea that no one in your neighborhood has used. Stir things up. Be unique.

• Imagine how height—whether it is a few inches or a few feet—might visually impact the beauty and feel of your garden.

• At your local grocery store, pick up a cardboard flat used for delivery of soda/pop/beer cans. The dimensions are approximately sixteen inches long by two inches high by ten inches wide. In the garage, or in an area where you can afford a little mess, do this exercise. Add a few inches of play sand (imaginary soil), a few various-sized stones, which represent imaginary structures or plants, and some small sticks that might be used as trees, fences, or paths. Pretend this is your garden on a very small scale and let your imagination go wild, as you move and play with the

also been very functional, providing easy access for wheelbarrow loads of soil, plants, and other garden items. More private or shyer gardeners may want to install a gate of some kind wherever they have such a gap. But do consider the idea of access and flow from one section of the garden to the next. My open approach has worked for me. I suggest that you do what feels most comfortable to you.

Cozy Garden Rooms

My individual garden rooms took quite awhile to evolve. In the beginning and before I was awakened by the gardening bug, my landscape was totally flat, unless I took into

elements. You can create paths, flower beds, walls, fences, and berms. With only a wave of your hand across the sand, you can erase one "plan," repeating the process many times. Practice this for one-half hour or so, and see what ideas you can generate. Some may get your creative juices flowing so much that you'll want to translate them to the "real" garden. (Thanks go to Panayoti Kelaidis for passing this idea on to me. I use it as a teaching tool in many of my classes.)

• If you're heading out on a shopping spree and you see an area that needs attention, grab your weeding tools, without even changing your outfit, and begin; the mall can wait.

• When you are working in your garden, keep an eye out for suckers sprouting from the feet of shrubs you are fond of. Even though it might not be an ideal time to move anything because of intense heat, or the best time to move plants has passed, take action anyway. Get a trowel and move these suckers all around your garden. Water them in well, and try to remember to keep an eye on them. In a few short weeks, the suckers will be new shrubs growing on their own.

• Act impulsively when working in your garden. Don't be concerned as you flit about and weed one section, and ten minutes later move to another section, even the first not yet "finished." When bored with one area, move on. Follow an internal order; avoid a regimented system.

• Tools: Don't be overly concerned about keeping tools organized or cleaned in your shed or garage; just feel lucky that they are returned after use! When you're weeding or planting and you need a certain tool, don't be fussy, settle for whatever will work at the moment.

• Don't adhere to rigid planting schemes or plant in straight rows. Arrange plants randomly and rely on a good inner sense as to which plants look good together. Trust your hunches and your eyes.

• Try one or more of these stimulating ideas. The next week or month, experiment and try another. Such ideas act as building blocks that will encourage your intuitive imagination to soar. ■

account the backdrop of the foothills miles away and the slope to a main road that sits forty feet above my back property line. For one full season, I hauled away debris (more specifically, concrete) that had been dumped years ago by inconsiderate builders. As I quietly cursed them and slowly removed the concrete chunks, I contemplated how to work some magic there.

As my mind flashed on images, I gradually formed mental pictures of ways to change my flat-as-a-pancake terrain. Architectural structures were desperately needed. Paths and rock gardens, walls and patios, almost instantly brought dramatic results to the previously uninviting landscape. (Of course, as you might imagine, installation of these elements was not instantaneous!) Rock gardens that changed elevation and paths that now meander throughout the garden capture the native feel of the land.

To create these rooms I first imagined height in one of my back corners. As I devoured garden books and looked at many local gardens, I noticed that rock was popular, and I found it attractive. As a member of the local North American Rock Garden Society, I had also seen many diverse styles of rock gardens. Because I wanted to be able to view all the plants easily, I envisioned a four-foot-wide path encircling my back rock garden. But I still wanted a shrub border and perennials behind the rock garden, so my second artistic vision was to leave a large swath for these plants, which would back up to the fence along my property line.

Before building my rock garden, I hauled soil into this area and, with my handy truck, which I was now using for a gardening business I had begun, I drove in a few loads of compost. (See the sidebar "Transforming Soil: Alchemy in the Garden" on page 22 for a more detailed explanation of soil amending and building a rock garden.) After the compost was turned under, the fun began—shopping for and installing the plants. Toward the back fence where I wanted more height, I planted *Betula occidentalis* (Western river birch), *Viburnum lantana* (wayfaring viburnum), and a few tall grasses. In the middle of this border I installed the shrub *Aronia melanocarpa* (black chokeberry), which has brilliant fall color, and surrounded it with perennials. In one corner, much too close to a path, I planted *Crataegus ambigua* (Russian hawthorn), forgetting that it potentially would be a twenty-foot tree! I transplanted it from elsewhere in the garden in early May, and it still bloomed with lovely white flowers at the end of the month.

While attending to this primarily shrub garden, I imagined how other garden rooms could be shaped, mentally separating each area loosely into dryland beds, perennial borders, rock gardens, paths, and so on. These secondary divisions helped me focus my attention on what possibilities there were within each. Next to the shrub border, there is now a garden framed by a long wall, where most of the plants are Western natives and other drought-tolerant selections. Many penstemons, unnamed sedums, and silver-leaved plants grow here, as well as irises and a well-branched *Chamaebatiaria millefolium* (fernbush). A favorite shrub of mine in this area, which will eventually grow twelve feet tall, is *Elaeagnus commutata* (silverberry). I mail-ordered it five years ago, so it is still quite small. This stiff, upright shrub has showy, wide, silver leaves and makes an excellent specimen. It can also be used as a screen, since it is somewhat twisted and dense. In front of the rock garden is a large perennial planting, which includes a dozen shrub roses, many ornamental grasses, and a few taller trees added in just the "right" spots to lend verticality. Jutting out from this area is a small, thumb-shaped bed surrounded on three sides by a gravel path. Where it slopes down, I always plant a patch of the choice, low-growing annual verbena 'Imagination', which blooms continuously with violet-purple flowers until the first hard frost. For variation, and planted exactly in the center of this bed, is the tall and large grass *Saccharum ravennae* (plume grass or hardy pampas grass). Its elegance commands attention in fall, winter, and summer, from wherever I stand in my garden, making this an intimate garden room with an extravagant accent.

Even though my garden contains a dozen garden rooms filled with hundreds of different plants, the whole area doesn't look like a kaleidoscopic circus. This is because I use restraint as an instrument of design. That is to say, I trust my intuition, but I don't let it go hog wild. For example, I love gray foliage plants; my eyes are drawn to their smoky color and the punctuation they bring to the garden. However, I wouldn't like an all-silver garden. I agree with Beth Chatto, who said in her 2000 book *Beth Chatto's Gravel Garden*, "Too many greys, herded together, can resemble an ash-heap." Similarly, I am madly in love with ornamental grasses, but they need varied companions for contrast. The straight or wavy lines of grasses against globular rose blossoms and other diversely shaped perennials, such as lavender, coneflower, and geranium, help accentuate the structure of both plants.

I also incorporate ideas and elements that I see in the wild plant communities of our foothills and surrounding mountains. I may find a lonely, stunted evergreen engulfed by pools of wildflowers, or a stony path that suddenly shifts from narrow to wide and back again, or a steep bank that challenges me to climb up and carefully zig-zag down. As well as the design elements I experience in these places, I use some of the plants I see there. I also bring in exotic plants from far-off lands such as Europe, China, and the Mediterranean, and combine them all so that they seem to naturally weave themselves together into a unified whole. My eyes and heart tell me where to place a rock or to plant a vertical specimen so that it will enhance my landscape, intuitively repeating what I see in the foothills and the high country. Again I rely on an inner hunch to know just what to do.

Small rooms break up a large garden into intimate spaces and allow the gardener to develop each space as a complete and specialized planting. For instance, a gravel path runs and widens between my shrub border (one garden room) and the rock garden (a second garden room). But from a distance these two distinct rooms seem to melt together, appearing to be a single lushly layered garden. Various tall spiky plants, textured perennials, and shrubs in the rock garden behave like a thin, veiled screen. From one perspective they are the main characters. Upon closer examination, you'll see that there is a second wave of tall plants in the background; yet each plant can quite satisfactorily be seen from a distance.

Hardscape of any kind behaves like a dancing partner for plants. Sometimes both are needed for a glitzy performance. As I move along gravel paths that twist and turn through

Amidst heavy boulders, a fusion exists among the large *Crataegus ambigua* (Russian hawthorne) in the background, the flowing blooms of *Aurinia saxatilis* (basket-of-gold), and the spiky flowers of *Salvia candidissima* (sage).

The white mound of *Chamaebatiaria millefolium* (fernbush) takes center stage as
Festuca glauca (blue fescue) highlights its wispy plumes among smooth and round boulders.

the garden, transporting me from one room to the next, I am attracted to unique details within each one. A small silver sundial or the smooth, shiny texture of a rock that sparkles when hit just right by the sun may catch my eye. The finely formed leaves of sages, evergreens, and other delicately shaped plants balance themselves against long and short walls jam-packed with plants of all kinds. Drifts of perennials are punctuated by shrubs and small trees. Sometimes I see these various elements individually. At other times they merge together as a whole.

Precious Stone

Rocks in some form or another have been integrated into gardens and landscapes for many centuries. During Roman times and probably before, when grottoes—those dark, gloomy, wet caves—were adjuncts to gardens, rocks have played a substantial role in creating harmony. In Greece and other countries in the Mediterranean region, caves were a welcome relief from the fierce sunshine. During the Renaissance, Italians built elaborate architectural designs with stones and water features, the rigid geometry of the stonework contrasting with the free forms of flowing water and trees. In some earlier cultures, when people built and worshipped extravagant stone structures, stone was seen as godlike. In other cultures, such as the Japanese, rocks were integral parts of a peaceful yet dramatic gardening style.

The English gardener William Robinson was well known for his eccentric and unruly style of gardening. In his book *The Wild Garden*, first published in 1895, he wrote a chapter entitled "Wild Gardening on Walls, Rocks, or Ruins," in which he stated: "There are hundreds of mountain and rock-plants which thrive better on an old wall, a ruin, a sunk fence, a sloping bank of stone, with earth behind, or a 'dry' wall than they do in the most carefully prepared border." An American contemporary of William Robinson's, Louise Beebe Wilder, was also a strong advocate of using rocks in the landscape. In her 1933 book *The Rock Garden*, she suggested getting ideas and inspiration from one's surrounding environment. In my locale, we look to mountainous areas to get ideas about rock types and naturalistic placement.

The tradition that Robinson and Wilder promoted has surfaced again. Currently there is an enormous surge, locally as well as nationally, to use rocks in the garden. Their rough and robust back-to-nature presence, along with their odd, individual shapes, whether formal or informal, makes them highly adaptable to today's gardens. The heaviness of rock, when combined with the etherealness of plants, creates a visually satisfying pairing of opposites.

The burgeoning popularity of stone is noted in an article in the December 2000 issue of *Fine Gardening* entitled "Stone Adds Naturalistic Structure to Any Garden." The author, Steve Silk, an avid gardener, shows how stone and plants form a graceful union and how the overall garden is enhanced by these two diverse elements. In the latter part of 1998, *The Wall Street Journal* (of all papers!) ran an article entitled "Rocking Your World," which described how wealthy homeowners are spending huge sums of money planting boulders on their properties. Some believe the practice may be a phase, but landscape designers think rock will continue to be fashionable because of its seeming agelessness and the way in which it accentuates the garden. The same article stated that a survey by the American Landscape Contractors Association reported that three-quarters of those landscapers who responded offer stonework to their clients. Homeowners are using rocks for nearly every purpose: seating, birdbaths, waterfalls, and simply focal points in the garden. The natural look is in and chic, whether you spend big bucks to construct your own grotto or just a few bucks on some pleasing boulders.

The idea for the shape of my thirty- by twenty-foot rock garden surfaced after a trip to Germany, where I saw fabulous old gardens in Munich and Berlin. Both the Botanical Garden of Göttingen University and the Botanical Garden of Justus-Liebig University, located in Giessen, which dates from the sixteenth century, impressed me tremendously with their comprehensive collections of alpine plants. But it was the ancient rocks in Giessen that brought the past into the present for me. In parts of this garden the rock was very weathered and worn, with dark markings and deeply etched grooves. Plants swept over the stone, bringing the archaic scene to life. At the Botanical Garden of Göttingen University, I admired an ancient-looking granite path that meandered through one of many artfully designed rock gardens. It was slightly curved and tapered, and its irregularly shaped stones, though flat and easy to walk on, did not tie too perfectly into each other. So it looked native and earthy as it separated two raised mounds of rocks and plants. I wanted to incorporate a portion of this style into my garden. I had always seen a path around a rock garden, never anything woven directly through the middle. It struck me as a unique concept.

As I continued to walk leisurely through these gardens, shifting my attention from side to side, I drooled over colorful "cushions and buns" nestled among the stones. These whimsical terms are commonly used by seasoned rock gardeners when they describe plants with curious features, such as tightly matted foliage or rounded, massed foliage elevated a few inches off the ground and looking like fancy embroidered pillows that might decorate the living room sofa.

Upon my return to the States, I began a diligent search for precious stone to pair with the cushion and bun plants I had admired at Giessen. I went to stone quarries, marking large and small rocks that I felt would fit the imaginative picture of my future garden. Granite rock, with smooth, angular, gray and pink lines running through it, was pleasurable. I also picked out some stones whose surface was speckled and rough, and others with big blotches of pink and gray. Some rocks were shiny and appeared to sparkle a bit—I definitely grabbed a couple of those. A few measured four or five feet across and two feet wide and weighed in at a ton or two. I arranged for the delivery and placement of those large boulders, but I also selected stones that I could lift by myself or with the help of one other person.

Creativity began as, along with two helpers, I separated large rocks from small ones. I used about ten boulders that needed to be placed by machinery. One person drove the front-loader as I directed him verbally and with the use of my hands and arms to the precise spot where I wanted the rock placed. I would continually tell him to shift to the left or right, or say, "Let's do this one again, with a different angle showing." Or I might say, "Shove this one deeper," or "Raise this one out of the soil more." It was not a quick process; patience and many hours were needed to get the look I wanted. With the smaller stones, I developed skill at sinking or pushing them into the ground, usually burying them by at least one third. I enjoyed creating a tumbling and natural effect. In fact, I was imitating Mother Nature, juxtaposing one rock against another. A few rocks grouped

In the foreground is an unknown yellow daisy. Moving clockwise is the fast-spreading aster 'Professor Kippenberg'; the white daisy *Boltonia asteroides* 'Snowbank' (Boltonia); *Sacharrum ravennae* (hardy pampas grass) skyrocketing in the center; and rose 'Golden Wings' peeking into the picture on the far right.

together can be eye-appealing, especially once the plants surround them and creep through and over their solid forms.

I would space my rocks anywhere from three inches to a foot or two apart, sometimes even more. When a few rocks are joined or almost touching, a plant pocket is created. Plants can cling to the surface of rocks, curl and snuggle up against them, even grow out of them! I learned that there are no hard-and-fast rules for rock placement, and I placed boulders in ways that caught my fancy. Sometimes, for variety's sake, I practically covered the rock with soil, allowing only a few inches to remain above ground. Other times the rock was huge, and I let a large portion remain visible. But I always made sure the best surface of the rock was facing the sky or just the right way to please me. Oftentimes, I randomly left a few gaps so that I could mass many plants of one variety together. And, like an artist unfolding her creation, I would stand back a few feet to admire what I had done, or to see where shifts and adjustments were needed. I discovered that adding rocks of various sizes, shapes, and colors brought differing forms and contours to my landscape.

As I was placing these stones, in one particular area I came across a small rock that especially appealed to me. It was totally round on the surface but was flat-bottomed, red, and very smooth. I placed it along a path with only its smooth surface visible. Now, many years later, it is enveloped by greenery. Yet I remember the pleasure of "planting" this particular stone.

A word of caution here: However you place boulders, be concerned with their stability. Burying about one third of a rock below the surface will help, but make sure it is secure and doesn't shift under your weight. Whether your berm is three feet or eight feet high, tripping on unstable rocks can be hazardous.

As lovely and aesthetically pleasing as rocks are, I believe that it's best to place the emphasis on the plants that join and soften them. When plants and rocks are united, a great partnership emerges between these two distinctly different yet compatible elements that

The cupped white blooms of *Cerastium alpinum* var. *lanatum* (woolly mouse ears) snuggle up to
the highly textured and red tones of Sempervirens ssp. (hens and chicks).
Adding appeal to the scene is the sun-colored Physaria sp. (bladderpod) and the small stones.

coexist so effectively in nature. Rocks, with their unpolished look and their diversity of character, provide a permanent background to the landscape and bring needed solidity against the softness of the plant material. Because of their density and neutral tones, rocks provide a resting place for the eye amidst the bustle of foliage and flower. And rocks create mystery in the landscape. What is planted to the side of a boulder or across the path? What is hidden in back of it? My curiosity is stirred every time I walk through my garden. I like to peek over a rock and be pleasantly surprised by what I see there.

Opposites attract. In the same way that people with clashing personalities are attracted to each other, rock seems to call for plant material and vice versa. Boulders afford structure, a sense of timelessness, and a unifying element that ties the garden together. They lend strength and support to my garden and provide windbreaks and moisture reservoirs for my plants. Finally, they allow me to bring a feeling of the surrounding grand geography into my small space. In short, I wouldn't garden without them.

My Specialized Soil Formula: In my large rock garden I have paid closer attention than elsewhere to soil mixture. It's not too extravagant a mix, just a bit different, so that it can accommodate a broad range of both rock garden plants and other perennials. It also serves plants that want little water. There is an exact recipe for this soil mixture; however, I usually follow it quite loosely, depending on my mood and the availability of ingredients.

I use equal portions of a gravelly material—either pea gravel or squeegee, which is also stone but about half the size of pea gravel—and a good garden loam or compost. These two are key ingredients, and I mix them in with my existing soil so that there are roughly equal amounts of all three elements. Pea-sized stone particles work well. They let moisture flow through so that plants are not sitting with their feet wet. Rock garden plants especially dislike that condition. If you have access to well-decomposed manure, it can be a fourth ingredient that works exceptionally well. But you will not face dire consequences if you do not use manure as a major ingredient for your rock garden. And most compost, bagged or bulk, has well-aged manure in it.

Putting a soil mixture together reminds me of a holiday cookbook I used when my children were young and my kitchen was often a bustle of activity. One recipe I used was for champagne punch: two bottles of 7-Up, one gallon of sherbet, and one bottle of champagne. The author wrote humorously that if the kitchen became too busy it wouldn't matter if an extra quantity of one of the items was added or a portion left out. The punch would always turn out to be delicious; all the party guests would enjoy it and, above all, each other. The metaphor works in the garden, too. Most plants are not terribly sensitive and perform beautifully without exact amounts of the above-mentioned ingredients. I like to strive for the soil composition that works for the widest range of plants. However, I also know that most plants tolerate variations in soil mixtures and still perform excellently. I am aware that in our mountains and in other plant communities around the world there are not equal proportions of soil, gravel, and organic matter. So I'm flexible.

Berm-Building: I like to garden in a loose and flowing manner; it makes gardening fun. As an intuitive gardener, I have no rules! I recall how a friend and I used to drive into my backyard in trucks loaded down with horse manure, which we obtained from the stable where she kept her horses. We would use heavy rakes to remove it from the trucks and then spread it to raise the ground to the level I wanted in a particular corner. If it was a warm winter day, when the snow had melted, leaving the ground quite soft, the trucks got stuck. When laying down wooden planks and digging around spinning wheels didn't help, AAA became a visitor to the garden. The trucks were rescued and the manure put in place. Even though the manure was "hot," I used it to build this berm and just waited a few months before I planted so as not to "burn" sensitive roots.

In the last berm I constructed, soil building was extremely serendipitous. I gradually added compost, small stones, and manure to elevate the mound slowly until I was satisfied with its height. I built the berm six feet tall, knowing that the soil would settle to about four feet. My soil recipe was not exact, but contained a little of this and a little of that. But, as I added amendments, I felt the soil constantly, being aware of its texture. I used my intuition and my eye, in addition to my fingers, in order to see what the soil was becoming and to make sure that the critical drainage factor would be satisfied. As I mentioned above, gravel of some kind is always a critical ingredient. I was pleased when the gravel and soil crumbled easily through my fingers. I was somewhat careful to make sure I didn't go overboard with either too much gravel or soil. But I was aware too that a little extra of either would definitely not hurt the survival of the plants that would be installed later on. It was a balancing act that worked successfully.

The Passion Blossoms

There are many trademarks of a passionate gardener. Planting throughout the year is one of them. Novice gardeners believe that planting begins in May and ends in July—or maybe in the fall, when a few more perennials can be tucked in. I plant nearly year-round—whether it's a shrub or perennial, whether the weather is cold or hot or anything in between. I believe most plants are better off in the ground rather than sitting and waiting for the ideal moment or the ideal weather conditions for planting.

Of course, there are exceptions to any rule. If the sun is baking the garden and I want to plant a delicate rock garden plant whose roots are just developing from a small container, I will be sensible, keep it well watered in its pot, and wait until temperatures cool down.

In spring and summer I watch the TV weather channel like a hawk. I like knowing what the outside conditions are going to be. What will my body have to deal with out there? When is it going to freeze or warm up or cool down? I'm not fond of hot sun beating down on me while I'm digging, planting, or wheelbarrowing yards of soil. I love cloudy, slightly cool weather with intermittent sun. Colorado and many other parts of the West are known for their abundance of sunny days, so my dream of cloud cover is not realized too often.

To escape the oftentimes relentless sun and heat, I frequently plant late in the season, saying to myself, "I'll plant this quickly," or "It's such a good sale," or simply, "This plant is

---

TRANSFORMING SOIL: ALCHEMY IN THE GARDEN

As an intuitive gardener, I am not overly fussy or scientific about soil. My garden is located a few miles from the foothills, and I discovered early on that my property was composed of clay: hard as a rock when dry, difficult to till or dig when overly wet. If mixed perennial beds were to succeed, I realized that the soil needed to change and large amounts of organic matter would have to be added. Now, exactly, what did I add? I brought in whatever I could find to gradually transform brown, icky, hard clay into dark, crumbly, almost "melt in your mouth" soil, which I named "chocolate cake."

Oftentimes my amendment was aged manure, compost, or just plain topsoil. (In areas with many native plants, though, I usually avoided doing any kind of soil amending.) Sometimes I had many yards of compost and manure delivered. Other times I had the landscape supply company mix up different combinations of soil products, such as four parts of screened fill dirt combined with six parts of rough cow manure. I wasn't too picky. I intuitively guessed how much I would need for a particular section, and it did not matter to me if there was too much; I could always make use of the excess in another spot or save it for the next season. On still other occasions I would drive to the landscape yard and, after inspecting large piles of assorted mixtures, would pick out the organic material that looked the choicest to me, often the one with a yummy dark brown color. I would then ask the yardman to dump a few scoops into my truck. Carefully and slowly I would drive down the highway,

---

irresistible and I must have it!" Truthfully, we in the West can plant successfully late in the season, but then winter watering is especially crucial because we can't depend on significant snowfall every year. Snow, an excellent insulator, protects plants like a blanket and helps keep the soil surface from drying. I do not mean just a dusting of snow, which is what we often get on the Colorado Plains. That amount doesn't count for much; it evaporates, melts, or blows away. At least a few inches is needed for beneficial cover and insulation.

Without this protection and moisture, and once the foliage dies back on herbaceous plants, there is root desiccation, and the entire plant might die, which you may not notice until spring. Winter winds, a common scourge in the West, come along and desiccate a plant even further, which can also contribute to its early demise. So if I reach out for those excellent fall plant sale items and plant them late, I pay special attention to their winter watering needs. During dry periods, when daytime temperatures reach fifty or sixty degrees Fahrenheit, not uncommon in the West, I drag out the hose and give these thirsty creatures a drink. If three or four weeks have gone by with no decent snowfall, I often water my entire landscape, including trees and shrubs. Here on the High Plains, winterkill

my truck overstuffed, hoping that my shocks and brakes would last a few more seasons! Knowing I was carrying a precious and expensive commodity—at least for a gardener—I hoped not too much of it would spill out from under my tarp and blow away.

In earlier years I had put together compost piles, casually layering grass clippings, kitchen scraps, soil, manure, and other assorted debris. Over time, the ingredients "cooked" and became well integrated. I then shoveled my homemade compost into various borders, and it worked beautifully. But things have changed. Now, perhaps after I have entertained and made a dozen deviled eggs, I may randomly toss the shells directly into my garden, having fun stomping and reducing them to tiny particles. I delight in knowing that they will disintegrate into the soil, but that is the extent of my "composting" efforts; these days, I prefer to buy the material pre-made.

My love affair with gardening begins with the soil. After all, soil is what activates the magnificent growing process in which seeds and small plants seem to magically transform. I love to move soil, improve it, dig and plant in it. It is the primary ingredient from which everything else springs. So, although I'm not very scientific about soil work, I am adamant about providing my plants with a suitable growing medium.

Making that rock garden, I once again felt as if I were an alchemist in an outdoor laboratory. Rather than using flasks, various liquids, and mostly inorganic materials, I work in the garden, creating—in whatever manner I choose—magical formulas with rocks, soil amendments, and plants. All their alluring facets of color, fragrance, and texture appeal to my senses. I am overjoyed with the transformation I have created. ∎

occurs most often not because of extreme cold but because plants dry out. Winter is often, but not always, dry. Warm daytime temperatures followed by cold ones at night cause further stress; plants can dry out during the day and then go into a freeze at night, causing damage to their root systems. Harsh winter sun, no longer filtered by the leaves of deciduous trees, is especially hard on anything evergreen—broadleaved shrubs and conifers alike. Wind simply adds insult to injury.

Plants used to regular irrigation during most of the growing season are especially susceptible to an early death unless a winter watering schedule is followed. Five minutes of hand watering on a balmy winter's day is not sufficient to thoroughly soak the root systems of most plants. I try to remember to soak each area from fifteen to thirty minutes once a month, circulating the hose around the garden to where the moisture is needed. Come spring I'm glad I attended to this chore.

A bonus of living in the West is that (aside from the more popular garden perennials) there is a host of plants I can be lax about when it comes to winter watering yet count on to return each year. Because they are native to our region, they instinctively know how to adapt and survive. Many, such as *Callirhoe involucrata* (wine cups or poppy mallow), have long, fleshy taproots that have the ability to store moisture when rainfall is scarce. Silver-foliaged plants such as *Artemisia frigida* (sand sage), with their light-colored, hairy foliage, reflect the intense sunlight and are not bothered by strong winds. Compact ground-hugging plants, like some species of *Achillea* (yarrow) and low forms of *Penstemon* (beardtongue), also escape high winds. Plants with succulent stems and leaves—the *Sedums* (stonecrops), for instance—also are winners in my garden because they store water in their leaves and can withstand long dry periods. In horticulture, though, there are always exceptions and variables. (Not all plants with succulent stems deal well with long stretches of dryness. Some forms of ice plant bloom nicely in low-water situations but can still need some irrigation if their stems go limp.)

Growth in Sophistication

On a recent early-spring trip out of town, I learned of a nursery nearby. I rushed over, saw a few desirable plants, and purchased them. They were items I could not find in my region unless I waited a few months and then diligently searched local nurseries. One of the plants I bought, although only a brief bloomer in early summer, had attracted me for years: *Paeonia tenuifolia* 'Plena', the fern-leaf peony. Its frilly, cupped, double red flowers and lacy foliage will forever thrill me. It did not matter that I had to drag this plant and others by plane and train to three other destinations around the country before I arrived home. I protected and coddled them so that I could eventually plant them safely in my garden.

Garden experts have their own ideas about how to garden or shop for plants. Some believe that before you go to a nursery you need to know what you want, *plus* know *where* you want to plant it once you have returned home. In spite of lofty plans and ideas, I believe that, like me, a great number of gardeners often buy spontaneously and plant what momentarily catches their eye. As we become more knowledgeable, we get more sophisticated about our choices. Instead of the fine blue-and-white flowers of our native *Aquilegia caerulea* (Rocky Mountain columbine), we now want *Aquilegia vulgaris* 'Nora Barlow', a cultivar with double pink-and-white flowers. (I especially like it because I have fond memories of a friend whose name is Nora; my intuitive mind links the friend with the plant.) Or perhaps instead of the everyday common iris, we develop a desire for *Iris pallida* 'Variegata', whose vertically striped, yellow-and-green swordlike leaves and purple flowers will contrast dramatically against a red brick wall.

As our tastes become more sophisticated, we become more discriminating. We want our gardens to look richer, golden and special, so that they describe our tastes at each moment, so that they say, "I like this; I don't like that." As I covet and search out the unusual or spectacular, I can admit to being bored with some plants. For example, the joy of growing petunias has mostly faded for me, no matter how full or double or colorful their blooms are. (However, when they are stuffed into a pot with other plants and greenery, they can indeed liven up an otherwise dull patio.)

I never did like *Cerastium tomentosum* (snow-in-summer), but before I became more worldly and knew of its aggressive tendencies, I planted it. Then I discovered *C. alpinum* var. *lanatum* (woolly mouse-ears). Out went the old and in came the new. This pixie-sized, white-flowered, gray-green mound stays where I've planted it—right next to a few unnamed hens and chicks with sculptured red foliage. These two plants make a great match, and neither invades its partner.

Another rise in my level of sophistication occurred with regard to *Delosperma nubigenum* (yellow ice plant). I've grown this familiar spring-blooming plant for years and will continue to do so. I like how it rolls over my pea gravel, caressing a huge spread of the silver leaves of *Santolina chamaecyparissus* (lavender cotton). But I have discovered *D. congestum* 'Gold Nugget', a recently introduced variety of ice plant. Its yellow flowers are larger than those of *D. nubigenum*, it blooms longer, and the blossoms are touched in the center with a nice dab of orange. This ice plant blooms from March to June and repeats sporadically in the fall. Its evergreen foliage stays tightly pressed against the edge of my granite wall.

The dainty flowers of *Campanula garganica* (bellflower) cling to and crawl up a massive boulder.

The genus *Corydalis* is yet another discovery. I like its ferny leaves and think of it as quite a highbrow plant. Cultivating a few of these definitely puts one in the upper echelons of horticulture! Its color forms are diverse: blue, pink, yellow, or white. Many species are not easy to grow, but in my experience average moisture, excellent drainage, and light shade are its requirements. Corydalis adds sparkle and intrigue to cool shade gardens. I've lost my share, especially the blue-flowered ones, so I stick with *C. cheilanthifolia* (bright yellow), *C. aurea* (pale yellow), and *C. ochroleuca* (white/pale cream). All three did well for me for years with minimal attention, although *C. aurea*, a biennial, disappeared after five years. I suspect it did not get enough moisture, even though others have told me it can tolerate somewhat dry conditions and blooms well in full sun. It was low, lacy, and not too vigorous in my garden. I'll probably try it again when I come across it at a nursery.

C. cheilanthifolia is not very well known in American gardens; I've rarely seen it at garden centers. Too bad, because it is large relative to other species in the genus. Petite yellow flowers rise out of a blue-gray rosette of intricate, needlepoint-like foliage. The plant blooms in early spring and can reach a height of fifteen inches in my region. When its blooming season is finished, the exquisite leaves ornament the front of my perennial border. Place its tiny foliage next to the dashing large leaves of any hosta or bergenia. I like the plant, but in this particular shady site it has become too content and needs a little roping in now and then; I simply pull it out or pot it up and give it to an up-and-coming highbrow gardener.

The pinwheel flowers of *Delosperma congestum* 'Gold Nugget' (iceplant)
are highlighted when tucked in among the rocks.

*C. ochroleuc*a is my pride and joy. It demands a lot of space, and I usually let it go until I see fit to again enlist a weeding tool. The elaborate network of foliage, which generally reaches a height of ten inches, and its delicate flowers, which bloom from late spring into fall, make it a treasure to grow. Because of its beauty, *C. ochroleuca* garners a lot of praise from visitors to my garden. This plant makes you proud to have climbed the ladder of sophistication.

Housekeeping

An undeniable fact of life among passionate gardeners is this: It's not only what's planted in the garden that is significant but also what gets eliminated, trimmed, or tweaked in some fashion. These fun chores take place in all seasons. And, yes, this kind of housekeeping is fun. The tidier gardeners among us (which I am sometimes) are meticulous about garden care and upkeep. It's our pride and joy. While nongardeners may be bored with trivial tasks such as weeding, we thrive on this opportunity to observe and be an active participant in the "goings on" in our gardens. The daily grind is not a grind at all. I enjoy an easy job such as snipping dead branches off a shrub to make it more attractive. I like to shear back the brown flowers of a clump of dianthus (pinks) so that I will be rewarded with yet another flush of color; yet even before the color reemerges in six weeks or so, the deadheaded grasslike dianthus foliage is attractive with its round, mat form and blue-green color.

I find weeding and light maintenance delightful, especially if the heat and bright sun are not too intense. It's a great relief to go outside after I have dealt with any kind of indoor duty. I'll grab a large bucket, my pruners, whatever weeding tool is handy, and, of course, a cushion so that I am comfortable. Sometimes I will focus on a small area and finish it; other times I'll be systematic and completely clean up a large area. Many times I jump from one activity to another. I'll sit for awhile, then I'll get bored and stand up. I'll browse my garden in search of another area that needs attention. In this next spot I may not sit down at all, hacking at weeds here and there, tossing them into my bucket or making weed piles randomly throughout my garden. (I learned this last technique from a friendly employee of mine, whose name was Pam. She never used buckets when she weeded. We laughed together as she made a trail of small weeds, which she would gather up later. We named these "Pam's Piles.") To weed is to relax.

A major housekeeping task is pruning. Passionate gardeners love to prune and usually have more than one pair of pruners to prove it. Aside from shovels and weeders, pruners are the most valued tools for many gardeners. I try to keep my pruners nearby, but if truth be told, many times I lose them. I'll place them on the ground, continue on with other activities, and promptly forget where I last saw them. Sometimes they stay out overnight; worse still, they may not get retrieved at all and become ruined by rain and snow. If I do find a well-rusted pair the following season, I clean them up and spray them with WD-40. I can usually salvage them for many more years of use—or until I lose them yet again! I know it's an important task to sharpen and clean tools over winter, but I'm rarely that organized. Nevertheless, I love a good pair of sharp, new pruners. I use them constantly to snip off old blooms, cut back perennials, and attend to the many jobs that are required when manicuring a garden.

Shrub roses, especially the large cultivars, are guilty of aggressive behavior and need to be pruned from time to time. During my novice years I mistakenly planted *Rosa* x *harisonii* (Harison's yellow rose—also known as "The yellow rose of Texas") too near a path, but because I like it as a backdrop to my rock garden, I haven't moved it. So it's necessary to get down on my hands and knees and almost do a hatchet job on it each fall or winter. My heavy-handed approach strongly thins this shrub from within and along the edges, cutting out old, diseased, or damaged wood and making more room for air circulation and sunlight. If my pruners are too small for this chore I will use a pair of loppers, a convenient tool for large garden chores. I know this treatment will encourage healthier blooms during the coming season yet give passersby peace as they tread along this path. I'm careful not to do an extreme amount of pruning because this rose only blooms for a few weeks in June, and if I prune too much in winter, I will eliminate the forthcoming flowers.

A watchful eye seeks out plants that aggressively roam garden beds or interfere with a bed's overall aesthetic effect. Constant pruning or digging out the aggressors keeps a garden looking fresh and performing at its peak in all seasons. Yes, some of these plants simply need to be dug and thrown out entirely. For instance, I had to remove all traces of *Galium odoratum* (sweet woodruff) from my garden. For quite awhile I liked this easy-care, white-flowered, shade-loving groundcover. But not any more. I was always pulling it out here and there until, finally, I relegated it to the compost heap, preferring to fill my garden with various forms of digitalis, hardy geraniums, and, finally, the more pleasing ground-cover *Lamium maculatum* 'White Nancy' (dead nettle). It doesn't spread like wildfire as long as I am careful not to give it too much water.

Not a spreader like sweet woodruff, but a nuisance nonetheless, are the short, svelte, green stems of *Genista tinctoria* 'Royal Gold' (woadwaxen), which randomly sprout all over one of my rock gardens. I like this yellow, summer-blooming three-foot shrub a great deal, and although disposing of its seedlings is a hassle, I am not quite ready to get rid of it.

Whenever I wander the garden with a sharp weeding tool, I am quick to chop seedling stems to the ground. But this shrub is useful because it protects my dwarf Norway spruce (*Picea abies* 'Little Gem') from sunburn. (Late in winter I cut down a few, but not too many, of the genista stems so that the spruce will have some breathing room.)

Another plant that has merit but requires a watchful eye is *Penstemon hirsutus* var. *pygmaeus*, which I have been growing for a number of years. Although it prefers partial shade, it is not bothered by the full-sun situation it resides in, mainly because it is at the bottom of a berm and receives enough water. In spring, this dwarf penstemon has pale lilac flowers. By late summer the wavy leaves are technicolored a deep maroon and dark green. Not naturally an aggressive plant, it spreads farther than I would like because of the extra moisture it is receiving. So I have found it necessary to rein it in, tossing out plants—yes, I admit I do that, but I also give many away—but leaving enough so that I can enjoy its splendid pale lavender color in spring and scarlet foliage in the fall.

One more plant that needs to be controlled is *Rudbeckia triloba* (black-eyed Susan). I like this Great Plains native for its yellow fall flowers with dark brown/black centers, borne on tall, stiff stalks. It energizes my fall garden, looking fabulous with rusty-red *Sedum* 'Autumn Joy' and any rose- or purple-flowered aster. For a number of years I let it seed around promiscuously, but this year, in mid-October, I had had enough. I thinned the number of plants and will continue to do so as I see fit.

A plant in my garden that has not looked happy recently is *Achillea ageratifolia* (Greek yarrow). This small relative of the common yarrow (*Achillea millefolium*) grows only three inches high and spreads more than a foot. For quite awhile it had a strong foothold in a large rocky berm, where it was cradled between two red granite boulders. There its gray dome of foliage produced a halo of white flowers. But it appears recently that another family has called this dome home. Ants. I saw the big gaps they had made in the center of the plant, damaging its look and curtailing its performance, so I knew it was time to replace the yarrow or to take cuttings and move them to other parts of the garden. It was a simple task to divide it; I just pulled the stems and foliage apart, pressed the divisions into the soil in other parts of the garden, and watered them in well. I eagerly await next summer to check out how successful my simplified propagating technique has been.

Joiners

Some passionate gardeners join clubs, while others quietly attend to their hobby in solitude. After a few years of volunteering for the Denver Botanic Gardens I joined the

North American Rock Garden Society, a group that is highly sophisticated in terms of plant knowledge. The members hold specialized plant sales and slide-show presentations, some given by speakers from around the world. Many NARGS members call themselves "plant pigs," a term used quite affectionately to describe their addictive behavior toward newly available plants. For example, if a sale is scheduled at 7 P.M., you can bet that by at least 6 P.M. ten members will be ecstatically waiting for the doors to open. Some might actually run to a sale table in order to be the first to grab a rare plant or one that is available in limited quantities. It's not always a pretty sight, but for many years I was one of them. (Well, I still am.) My enthusiasm even prompted me to become president of the club several years ago.

**Papaver anomalum album (poppy) with its buttery-yellow center
stands out well against the large textured green leaves of Salvia sclarea (clary sage).**

Some people become members of clubs but are picky about what tasks they wish to do. A club is always in need of cashiers, or someone to write out labels or sort plants for sale. As a club member you are able to choose the tasks that pique your interest. I have known people who were minimal gardeners but loved the social interaction, and I've known others who avoid social involvement and are members only to attend plant sales or to pick and choose rare seed from around the world. Personally, I have enjoyed the club experience. I like the one-on-one contact I get at monthly meetings as I chat with fellow gardeners and exchange ideas, seeds, and plants. This is where I learn about members' successes and failures with various plants and techniques.

Teaching

Teaching entered my life quite spontaneously. I had become tired of weeding and planting gardens for others, and I needed to express to other passionate gardeners what I had learned. I also felt that I wanted to experiment with something new and challenging. At a yearly garden event, which took place during a winter cold spell, I approached a professor of horticulture and nervously asked whether I could teach at his institution, a local community college. He listened as I described my gardening background. I sent him my résumé, and soon I found myself in the classroom, spouting what I believed to be the truth about rock gardens.

I relied on the teachings of Graham Stuart Thomas and his book *The Rock Garden and Its Plants* as well as H. Lincoln Foster's *Rock Gardening*. I also realized that my years of volunteering at the Denver Botanic Gardens Rock Alpine Garden were paying off. I continued to research the topic of rock gardens and gradually tailored my lectures and slide shows to focus on Western regional gardens. The students were interested, and I was overjoyed to be a part of their horticultural education process, which became yet another method of learning for me. I slowly developed a slide library to show pictures and discuss the huge spectrum of plant material that would work for these budding gardeners.

Latin Lover (Botanical, That Is)

Teaching began my ongoing love affair with botanical Latin. I enjoy studying the names, saying them, writing them. Because I am far from being a Latin scholar, I still savor being able to pronounce some of these "unpronounceable" words and, although a few are challenging to say, like a child's tongue twisters, I have grasped the technique so that the words roll off my lips rather easily. I find it fun, and joke about it with students who remark, "How do you learn all those complicated names?" I explain to them that if you love a subject, it's both invigorating and enjoyable.

Some gardeners like knowing the Latin names of plants, while others are perfectly satisfied with common names. There are pros and cons associated with each naming method. I'll begin by discussing Latin names. From making much use of the Denver Botanic Gardens library, I learned about Carl Linnaeus, the eighteenth-century Swedish naturalist who designed the biological classification system that is still used today. This international language is informative and complex when looked at from the angle of a botanist or a taxonomist. The genus name (the first element of a plant's botanical name) is capitalized and set in italics; it refers to a group of plants that are related in some basic way, either structurally or genetically, even though they may look very different from one another. A genus may contain thousands of different species or, in rare cases, only one species. The species name (also called the specific epithet), which is the second element in a plant's name, is set in italics but not capitalized. A botanical name may contain additional elements. Some species have been divided into subspecies (abbreviated as ssp. or subsp.), varieties (abbreviated as var.), and forms or forma (abbreviated as f.) and many popular plants have a myriad of cultivars. Cultivar names are set in roman type within single quotation marks.

Unfortunately, some people consider the use of botanical Latin to be elitist—and, truthfully, it does have a bit of that snobbery attached to it. However, I find it stimulating to learn about the genus, species, and variety of each plant to see what characteristics differentiate one kind from another. The important point to remember is that a Latin name, although it may be long and complicated, is the most reliable way to precisely identify a plant, whether in the garden, in the nursery, or in the wild. Every element of a Latin name conveys information about the plant.

I have found that as I navigate my way through botanical Latin, I learn a great deal about the plants themselves. An example is a particular species of spruce tree: *Picea pungens* 'Glauca Procumbens'. Each word tells me something about the plant. *Picea* denotes that it is a spruce and *pungens* means "sharp" or "pointed," as the needles of a spruce are. Glauca, part of the cultivar name, explains its blue color, and finally Procumbens refers to its trailing growth habit. Another illustration is the shrub *Rosa rugosa*. The species name *rugosa* informs me that this rose has wrinkled foliage. By touching and rubbing its leaves, I can experience this firsthand.

A little Latin can be misleading, though. It's easy to jump to conclusions, as I did for years with *Campanula garganica*. I thought I surely knew what this name meant in English.

The ferny foliage and reddish stems of *Rosa hemisphaerica rapinii* on the left are balanced against the dwarf spruce *Pinus cembra* 'Blue Mound'. The tawny tips of *Calamagrostis* x *acutiflora* 'Karl Foerster' (feather reed grass) in the background help accent the other large ornamental grass *Miscanthus sinensis* 'Strictus'. The orange flowers belong to the herb *Agastache ruprestris* (hyssop), and the sunny yellow flower is *Helichrysum splendidum* (strawflower).

Campanula was easy: The flowers within this genus are shaped like bells, and indeed "bellflower" is its common name. But for a long time I assumed that garganicus meant "large." This never made much sense, since this blue-flowered plant is dainty, clings to rocks, and does not grow to more than six inches in height. Then I finally uncovered the true meaning of *garganicus*; I learned that the species is native to Gargano, Italy. How fascinating!

A species name is often an adjective and will give the gardener some clue about the plant: how it looks, feels, or smells; how it will behave in the garden; where it originated. Two straightforward Latin names are *Rosa multiflora*, a rose that has multiple flowers, and *Ipheion uniflorum* (star flower), a bulbous perennial whose blue or white flowers are borne one per stem.

Some gardeners prefer common names to Latin ones. After I had studied botanical Latin, I read an article in the July 2000 issue of *The Garden* entitled "Am I a Latin Lover?" by Peter Seabrook. *The Garden*, which is the journal of the Royal Horticultural Society in England, is an excellent magazine and considered quite sophisticated among professionals, so I was surprised to see an article that favored common names (although a sidebar stated that the editors welcomed other viewpoints on the topic). Mr. Seabrook, for years a popular television host for international garden tours, believes that Latin is an obstacle to people's learning about plants. He has been in the business for over fifty years and finds it difficult to remember all the new names that keep surfacing, especially for ornamental grasses. He sympathizes with those who believe these names are not helpful to the everyday gardener and thinks that for many gardeners Latin is an instant turn-off. He notes that most people are happy to have "the blue flower," "the tall one," or "the variety, with purple flowers, that stays low to the ground." Such customers would be content if a nursery salesperson just said, "Plant this in sun and give it a lot of water." And that would be that. They don't want to be bothered with long, complicated names that are meaningless to them—enjoyment of the flower is their ultimate goal. Whatever that flower is to taxonomists, these people simply want something to admire as they walk out the front door heading to the neighbor's house.

I think that whether you use common names or Latin names is a matter of personal preference. Gardening is not everyone's all-consuming hobby or chosen profession. As a highly passionate gardener I have learned that, incredible as it may seem, others may not feel as I do. People find contentment when they plant a few petunias or grow annual geraniums or plant some mums. A little color around the patio satisfies them. For these people and many others, common plant names are adequate.

But using only common names can lead to confusion. Often there can be two, three, or more common names for one plant, depending on which part of the country you're from. If you go to buy a plant and ask for it by its common name, the salesperson may not know which plant you are referring to. Oftentimes plants are given cute names in order to make them more saleable, as they may have a sentimental tone or evoke touching memories, such as bluebells (*Campanulas*) or love-in-a-mist (*Nigella damascena*) or bleeding heart (*Dicentra*). As children we may have heard these names from our grandparents and neighbors, who loved to grow the old-fashioned flowers. These same common names may awake some desire to re-create the past in our gardens.

The situation can become troublesome, however, if you should ask for "butterfly weed" or "pleurisy root" and the grower has named the plant "gay flowers." The Latin name for butterfly weed is *Asclepias tuberosa*, and it is not a weed at all in the garden. But which name is most marketable: butterfly weed, pleurisy root, or gay flowers? The salesperson at the garden center may not have the slightest idea what you're talking about if you only use the common name. But if you state the complete Latin name he or she will know exactly what you want.

Or perhaps a customer requests a particular rose she has heard about, one that is thornless and blooms late summer into fall with a flower six inches across. It turns out that she is looking for rose of Sharon, which is not a rose at all. She would have had no problem if she'd asked for *Hibiscus syriacus*. (Of course, the other possibility in this scenario is that the person behind the counter may not know plants; that depends on how much good help the garden center was able to find for that particular season.) When you know a plant's Latin name, you can be sure that you are getting exactly what you want, provided the plant is labeled correctly. For instance, you may be shopping for a specific silver-leaved plant, *Artemisia pycnocephala* 'David's Choice' (sage), which is a mound-forming eight-inch sage and quite a specialty in gardening circles. The plant is remarkably different from *A. pontica* (Roman wormwood), which reaches twelve inches high, can be aggressive in moist soil, and is not as tidy-looking as 'David's Choice'. But both have gray foliage, and both belong to the genus *Artemisia*.

Yet another example is the genus *Penstemon* (beardtongue). (And, yes, part of the flower is tubular and looks like a tongue!) The genus contains more than three hundred species, many available at garden centers. A novice gardener may be comfortable, even thrilled, buying any one of them—perhaps he chooses the common Western native *P. strictus* (Rocky Mountain penstemon), with its blue-purple flowers. However, a more seasoned and knowledgeable gardener may already have five species and now doesn't want just any penstemon; she is looking for a particular one called *P. digitalis* 'Husker Red', a plant with white flowers and reddish foliage. Or perhaps this gardener has advanced to an even more unusual species named *P. murrayanus*, one with red flowers, which grows natively from eastern Texas into Louisiana. She is attracted to its unusual blue-green foliage and the fact that it is native to Southeastern states, therefore tolerating more moisture than some of the other penstemons. This gardener has a slightly moist spot in her garden for which *P. murrayanus* would be ideal. So, for some gardeners, it is important to get exactly what they want and to gather as much information as possible about each plant, while others are not fussy. I fall into the former category: I want to learn everything I can about the plant I am purchasing.

My final advice is "Do what works for you." Stick with common names if you like, or go down the winding (and sometimes taxing) path of learning botanical Latin. Whichever you choose, remember that gardening should be fun. There are plenty of other things in life that stress us, so if learning the Latin names of your plants becomes one of them, let Latin go and simply focus on making your garden picturesque, with abundant color and texture throughout the year.

Throughout this book I do use Latin names, but wherever possible I've tried to include the prevailing common names used in our region as well, so gardeners of any persuasion should be able to find their old and new favorites without too much trouble.

Crocus tommasinianus pokes through the seemingly vast soft leaves of *Verbascum bombyciferum* 'Arctic Summer' (mullein).

CHAPTER TWO

Everything Under the Sun

❧

*W*estern sun can be fierce. However, from my vantage point, lucky is the individual who has it in abundance. The sizzling and merciless heat of the summer does many people in, but for the passionate gardener it is a precious gift. As gardeners, we want gold and riches in our landscapes, and sun is a vital component of achieving them. We may wilt in, and whine about, the heat, but many of our plants thrive on and crave that intensity.

The selection of plants for sunny spots in the garden is huge, and the possibilities for creative combinations are endless. We

Above: On top of the berm—lavender flowers of *Salvia sclarea* (clary sage), the shimmering panicles of *Stipa comata* (needle and thread grass), and the airy blossoms of *Crambe cordifolia* (giant kale).

gardeners resemble painters: We can dip our brushes into a vast array of colors and tempting textures, unleashing luxurious potential in our gardens. Each grouping of plants has a palette of its own. Whether we want to grow sun-loving plants dry or with irrigation, our choices are many. Sunny sites offer us the pleasure of experiencing a huge variety of plants with striking foliage, as well as lively plant unions.

I love experimenting. I rarely know specifically what I'm looking for when I shop at a garden center. If it's early spring and I'm thrilled with something that's blooming in my garden, I may rush to the garden center and try to pick up more of it, knowing that the following spring I'll have oodles of what has excited me at that moment. As a result, even before most trees leaf out, my garden in early spring is densely packed with a mosaic of unusual flowers and plants with intricate foliage patterns.

Bulbs

By late winter, and even before, gardeners crave spring; we want to see bright purples and yellows, and we are delighted when the first crocus or snowdrop erupts through the earth. No matter how beautiful and restful winter is, we want to see spring light up our gardens! This feeling stirs throughout our bodies as we yearn to dig in the once-frozen soil and admire our successes, as well as take note of what may need replacement. We have had enough of leafless trees and indoor activities. Our patience has snapped! Smiles cross our faces as soon as temperatures warm to fifty for more than a day or two and we see green shoots poking through the soil.

Depending on how severe the winter has been and the location of my dwarf bulbs, different ones emerge at different times. Supposedly first in line to bloom is *Galanthus nivalis* (snowdrop). These can often be found piercing through patches of ice, as well as nestled close to tree trunks. There is also an elegant double-flowered counterpart, *G. nivalis* 'Flore Pleno'. These white, tear-shaped flowers sometimes bloom in tandem with *Eranthis hyemalis* (winter aconite), which is famous for its cute Elizabethan-style choker just beneath the bloom. When it's fully opened, any gardener who makes the effort to get down to ground level will be rewarded by its pleasant scent. Its yellow-cupped blossom is barely an inch off the ground, while those of *G. nivalis* and its double form sit a few inches higher. In some microclimates in my garden these flowers have bloomed as early as January; in others, they appear as late as March.

It took me a few years to discover that it's often necessary to soak *E. hyemalis* bulbs in a few inches of water overnight before planting. This simple technique protects them from shriveling up and disappearing entirely from the garden. This treatment might not be required if the bulbs arrive fresh at my door via FedEx straight from Holland, or if I plant them immediately upon arrival, but because I'm a lazy gardener, this seldom happens. Another important trick I learned is to plant them beneath deciduous trees; this also ensures that they do not dry out. Early on, when I planted them in sunny sites, they tended to fry in the hot summer sun, rarely returning the following year.

After these late winter/early spring flowers bloom, next in line, no matter the severity of the winter, are a few small species crocuses, all yellow with dark orange centers. Sometimes they even bloom before anything else because heat is reflected off the stone steps they are planted near, and they bask in sunny mornings. A week later, while the yellow crocuses are still at their peak, many others join the parade, including *Crocus tommasinianus* 'Ruby Giant', with its reddish purple color. 'Ruby Giant' is considered somewhat squirrel resistant. My husband is a squirrel lover. Right next to where these crocuses bloom, a squirrel feeder is nestled into the groundcover, and a few of these creatures are always dashing up and down our gigantic cottonwood. I'm grateful that, so far, they have not damaged any of the flowers I idolize.

As I approach my house, from almost a block away I see bunches of lemon-yellow crocuses, along with the purple varieties, like fresh outdoor bouquets, dotting my landscape. At this time, even though spring snows will certainly appear, bees know warm weather is upon us and swarm the crocuses, tucking their noses down to enter the flowers and seek out the nectar.

To unite perennials with crocuses, plant various shade-loving hellebores nearby. Many species of *Helleborus* are available; most are evergreen, but in cold climates like mine, the old foliage becomes rather worn and needs to be trimmed in late winter. Sometime between January and March, depending on snow and microclimates, new growth emerges. *H. orientalis* (Lenten rose), sometimes known as *H. x hybridus*, has dark green, slightly glossy, serrated leaves, with thin veins of burgundy through them. In my garden it reaches about a foot and a half high. Flower color can be white, pink, rose, or yellow-green.

Once considered a separate species, *H. atrorubens* has rich, plum-purple flowers and leafage. It is now usually classified either as *H. orientalis* subsp. *abchasicus* or as *H. orientalis* 'Early Purple'. All of the hellebores illuminate the landscape at a time when gardeners are practically begging for anything colorful. It is truly glorious to see their large, nodding, bell-like blooms in my region from January to May. They are slow to mature, but well worth the wait. After seven years, my small, mail-ordered *H. orientalis*, the rather common one with whitish yellow flowers, is a foot across, with fifteen blossoms. Generally, I don't mind waiting that long to have a sizeable plant to enjoy because, as spring moves along, there are many

The tiny flowers of *Draba parnissica* bake in this sun-drenched spot.

other flowers to admire! If you have the plum-shaded species, you might be fortunate and it will bloom in concert with a sea of *Eranthis hyemalis* for an exhilarating combination. The darker shades look marvelous interspersed with *Galanthus nivalis* as well.

Also exhilarating is the knowledge that over time hellebores, if they are happy and receive sufficient moisture, will spread and form colonies. Avid gardeners should know that breeders have developed many new cultivars in such colors as red, burgundy-black, and violet. There are also recently introduced varieties with extra-wide flowers, as well as those with a coating of silvery hairs and a bronzy tint, such as *H. odorus*.

As spring travels to my backyard and the ground gradually thaws, a few crocuses are poking up in bloom through *Ephedra minuta* (joint fir). This mat-forming gray-green evergreen has needle-thin leaves that dwarf bulbs can bloom around; occasionally they even spring through the foliage. Early-blooming crocuses are also a welcome sight when they make their way through the pillowy maroon mounds of *Armeria maritima* 'Rubrifolia' (sea pink or thrift). This last scene is even more dramatic because the plants back up against a foot-high slab of smooth, mottled granite.

After most crocuses have passed, there is barely a pause before garden activity is in full force. Because I use mostly intuition as to where I plant many of my perennials and bulbs, I'm delightfully surprised when I see a cohesive melding of plants that are stirred together just "right." In one area, where there are dwarf bulbs and perennials, I see a ribbon of colors drifting through. What catches my eye initially is *Iris* 'Scribe', a six-inch gem streaked purple and ivory. I'm heartened to have this miniature dwarf bearded iris, which I likely purchased at a plant sale years ago. It's a vigorous grower, which I dig up and replant around my garden every few years. Next is *Alyssum montanum* (mountain basket-of-gold), also low in stature, with small rounded balls of yellow flowers. *Tulipa clusiana* var. *chrysantha* and *T. batalinii* 'Bright Gem' are two excellent diminutive bulb choices that appear in this twisted river of color. The first is crimson and yellow, and I'm glad it has naturalized over time. Beneath it, and blooming a few weeks later, is a dianthus whose species I don't know, with pink flowers and a tight, cushiony shape. In recent years I've been attracted to the various

**Amidst the wire-thin and wiggly foliage of *Ephedra minuta* (joint fir),
Crocus tommasinianus shows its face to the sun.**

cultivars of *Tulipa batalinii* because of their wavy foliage as well as their wonderful blooms. 'Bright Gem' has soft, sulphur-yellow flowers. This area is covered with red and gray pea gravel, adding a dash of hardscape material that casually bonds all these plants together. Two other dwarf bulbs to try are *Tulipa tarda*, which in a few short years will multiply and make a nice splash across your landscape, as well as *Tulipa Kaufmanniana* 'Ancilla', a large, white-flowering bulb colored red and deep yellow in the center.

Not far from this spot is an explosive combination that brings together bulbs and bold foliage. After a number of years, *Verbascum bombyciferum* 'Arctic Summer' (mullein) has begun to surface in a few spots around my rock gardens. Generally this mullein pleases me; if too many seedlings appear, I catch them when they're small and remove them. The large (up to a foot long) silver leaves swim over my pea gravel. Since I am always planting bulbs, particularly crocuses or alliums of some kind, a few crocuses have multiplied and grow sporadically wherever they choose. Some have popped up between the leaves of the verbascum, looking quite elegant in shades of pale lavender with refreshing yellow stamens tipped with deep orange pollen. In fact, some have even ripped through the leaves in their strong desire to bloom.

The crocuses' strong desire to bloom goes hand in hand with my love of seeing them in full bloom the following spring. I never buy specific amounts or certain kinds of bulbs. I just wait to see which mouth-watering descriptions and perky colors entice me. Some I order through catalogs in bulk—one hundred, two hundred, or several hundred at a time. Other times, perhaps after Halloween when I'm driving near a local nursery (how accidental!), I'll automatically stop by to see what juicy bulbs they are selling. On the spur of the moment, I'll buy a few handfuls, or even a few bags full! I usually stick with dwarf bulbs, because the typical early-spring or late-winter storms Colorado receives ruin the larger tulips and daffodils. Another plus to dwarf bulbs is that I don't need to dig big, deep holes, and a third is that I prefer these petite blooms.

Troughs

Along with early-blooming bulbs, troughs usher in spring. They are excellent features in a sunny area, whether the garden is large or small. A trough is a container made of some stonelike material, usually with one or more quarter-inch holes in the bottom for drainage. Such a receptacle is ideal for small plants—that is, those under approximately six inches. If these smaller plants were planted directly in a large rock garden or perennial garden, they might seem to disappear among the flowers of the larger plants. By using complementary dwarf plants in a trough, one can create a complete garden community in a limited space.

Originally, most true troughs in this country were large cement feeders for cattle. But these are a rarity to find now. In recent years, as access to these stone troughs dwindled, gardeners (most often rock gardeners) developed look-alikes made of a material dubbed "hypertufa." Recipes vary but are basically a combination of portland cement and peat moss plus perlite or vermiculite, sometimes with sand added. Hypertufa troughs are porous and lighter in weight, and often smaller in size, than the heavy stone ones (of course, that is without the soil mixture and plants). If you don't have a trough and don't want to invest in one, you can design and build your own; check your local botanic garden or garden center for classes.

Troughs come in various sizes and shapes; most are rectangular, though you'll find round and oval ones too. Site them where you can enjoy them up close: next to an entryway, on top of a low stone wall, on steps, or even, as I have done, in the garden itself. Approaching my front door is a raised, curved flagstone path ending in steps. A few of my troughs rest on these steps, where houseguests can admire them as they enter. Others are in my back rock garden, staged on big boulders, or at the edge of my patio. For better viewing, some gardeners even build their own pedestals out of stones, bricks, or whatever spare material is available.

Like the rest of my gardening practices, I keep trough gardening simple and spontaneous. I don't get frazzled with complicated soil mixtures but rely on my good intuition. My technique is similar to cooking—a little of this, a little of that, and voilà—a crafted masterpiece! On top of my soil and gravel mixture, which is roughly one part soil and two parts pea-sized stones, I anchor a few small rocks, mimicking a large rock garden. Sometimes I keep the planting site flat, equal in height to the edge of the trough, which might be anywhere from four to twelve inches high. Other times I raise the planting level a few inches, reproducing the effect of a mini-mountain range. Whatever designs my riotous artistry comes up with, my major focus is the plants. I want them to shine through, taking center stage.

Topping the entire trough is a thin layer of pebbles. This material can vary in size from quarter-inch to half-inch or larger, depending on what appeals to you. This mulch has several functions: It's a weed inhibitor, it's an attractive layer that flatters the plants, and it helps hold the soil mixture together well so that plants and stones don't wash away when they receive moisture. My troughs are rarely watered, receiving only what Mother Nature provides and an occasional sprinkle from the hose when I water another area. (Winter watering may be necessary, depending on the location of the troughs, the amount of snow we receive, and the maturity of the plants.)

The narrow grasslike foliage of *Tulipa tarda* helps to accent the bicolor flower.

Some of my troughs are elaborately planted, while in others I have limited my selection to hens and chicks (*Sempervivum* ssp.), whose complex textures and traits are glorious, even when they are not blooming. Growing slowly, like icing dripping over a warm frosted cake, the minute foliage and flowers of these plants gradually drape themselves over the gray stone edge.

In one trough I have an annual, *Androsace lactiflora* (star dust rock jasmine), that originated in Siberia and Mongolia. Over a number of years, it has become well established in this oval container, since it is a reseeding annual. More aristocratic gardeners may shun this plant, thinking it is picayune because it is so small. Maybe the fact that it returns with a splash each year pleases me. In my garden, I notice its one-inch, red-tinged rosettes in winter, spreading their delicate foliage over the small stones. As the season creeps forward between spring storms, the foliage mutates to green and out pop needle-thin stems a few inches long. Within a week, at the tips of these stems, tiny five-petaled white flowers with hints of yellow at the center appear. The rosette stays intact, while the airy flowers flutter about when any wind comes along. In this same container, and contrasting with the delicate form and airy habit of the androsace, is *Orostachys spinosa*, also known as *Sedum spinosum*.

Orostachys spinosa often gets mistaken for a sempervivum, more commonly known as a hen and chick, because of its small size and also because the two plants look a bit alike. But upon close inspection it is quite different. The unusual characteristics of this particular orostachys make it a real winner for a trough or small rock garden. It forms dense clusters, tightly packed together, rising up to four inches and stretching out, over a number of years, to double that width. These rosettes appear a tad spiny, with sharp points at their tips, but they can be gently touched if one is careful. When all the rosettes are crowded together, they look much like scoops of ice cream on a hot summer's day. Once the rosette flowers it dies, but it leaves many so-called babies to continue the cycle. The flower stalk itself can reach twelve inches high, with sophisticated patterned scales coating the spike. Small, whitish green flowers tightly circle the stem in spring. But this plant's striking elements are its texture and foliage, which reign supreme in my garden. As the foliage deteriorates and turns brown in late summer, additional puffy succulent spikes spring up, without any coaxing whatsoever, and the plant delightfully reblooms in the cooler fall months.

Further into spring, but still before my large cottonwood leafs out and while my androsace is still in flower, I enjoy *Draba rigida* (bun draba), which passionate rock gardeners call a cushion plant. I vaguely remember hearing about drabas when I volunteered at the Denver Botanic Gardens Rock Alpine Garden. When I saw this inch-high plant, I imagined it might look good in one of my containers. Securely planted in a fifteen-inch-diameter round trough, it is shaped like a small sweet roll that one might indulge in for breakfast. When it's out of bloom, I can't resist patting this emerald green bundle with the cup of my hand; it's so cute! I am reminded of when I, along with Panayoti and fellow rock gardeners, hiked through the Rocky Mountains. I laughed with pleasure as I patted many round and cushion-shaped alpine plants with my palm. Jokingly, Panayoti began to call this motion the "Raff pat"! As the species name indicates, it is rigid and tight, yet slightly giving to the touch. I relish seeing this plant year-round at the foot of my front door, as I enter and leave my house. It blooms for a few weeks in early spring, capping the mat with a multitude of tiny yellow flowers, which rise a few inches above the evergreen foliage. I have two of these drabas next to each other and after a number of years their foliage naturally knitted together. That looked great for awhile, but when some of the foliage began to die out in spots, I learned that these plants do not like to be crowded. I cleaned out the dead foliage, and they seem to have recovered.

Many of these small cushiony and mat-forming gems are also at home tucked into planting pockets in a dry stone wall, along paths where their distinctive fabric can be seen, and, of course, among any rocks that may be on your site. Here is where your intuition can blossom; plant these cute critters wherever you see an open space that looks inviting for something green and growing.

Good drainage, preferably with small stones in the mixture, and light watering are two critical features when you're growing these somewhat delicate plants. There are three hundred different drabas, mostly with flowers in shades of yellow. For the sake of brevity, I'm suggesting only two additional species, both delectable: *D. repens* and *D. parnassica*. The first is very low, creeps, and produces yellow flowerheads on short, wiry stems above buns of tiny green leaves. The second one is an inch or so taller but still cushiony and produces bright yellow flowers in early spring. I was curious as to where the species name parnassica came from. My research led me to a small book called *Gardener's Latin* by Bill Neal, a delightful publication that explores the origins, lore, and meaning of a host of botanical names. I soon discovered that there is a Mount Parnassus in Greece and that *D. parnassica* grows there, as well as on the Balkan Peninsula among mountain rocks.

A tiny plant that I have enjoyed growing for years in my troughs is *Lewisia pygmaea* (pygmy bitterroot). It is native to the southern Rockies, where it can be found in rock crevices. It grows to about three inches high, with fleshy, pencil-thin green stems. Up to a dozen succulent tufted stems bathe in sunshine on the pea gravel as they fold gently over the edge of the trough. The pinkish, half-inch flowers bloom toward the center of the plant. It likes cool weather, blooming in early spring and repeating sporadically in fall. I am glad it has spontaneously seeded itself in another one of my troughs. To prolong its life, I generally keep it dry in summertime. I like contrasting the long narrow stems with the solid, round shapes of sempervivums that I have indiscriminately let multiply in some of my troughs.

I strongly encourage trying troughs. They offer diversity in the world of gardening, compared to larger plants and the more traditional perennial borders. Over the years I have discovered there are many people who just love the tiniest flowers. Through experimenting with troughs, the gardener can have these adorable plants, many with almost microscopic flowers and foliage.

Focus on Foliage

A key phrase in the world of home real estate is "Location, location, location." This truism emphasizes that the inside of a house, even if meticulously designed, is often not as important as the major factor of placement in the neighborhood, including closeness to schools and access to major shopping centers and highways. A similar rule applies in a garden, although the cast of characters is obviously different. Color is valuable, but for long-lasting effect, one needs "Foliage, foliage, foliage" and "Texture, texture, and more texture!" These two features are critical for gardeners who want to liberate new ideas in the garden and extend interest from season to season.

Don't get me wrong: I adore color and show-biz theatrics, but it's impossible to overstate the staying power and effectiveness of foliage and evergreen plants, rose hips, and various berries, as well as suitable hardscape elements, all interwoven. It is the spellbinding relationship of all these parts to each other that achieves a sensational visual presentation. But how does one get these combinations? Personally, I'm not afraid to experiment. I trust my hunches and imagination. Combining opposites, along with relying on my intuition, is the major clue to exploring the latent possibilities of plants. Some of the complementary qualities I make use of are rough against smooth, big against small, flowing against upright, and broad against finely dissected. Diverse colors are also significant: blue paired with gray, gray against green, and so forth. My boulders and smaller rocks, when paired with plants, offer much opportunity in contrast. To produce beautiful pictures, I maximize these ideas, planning for breathtaking results.

My garden is large, so it can handle high-powered and diverse characteristics without looking like a circus. I use such plants as *Crambe cordifolia* (giant kale), which grows five feet high and showers my garden with a huge smokescreen of tiny white flowers and rippled, greenish blue leaves that grow over a foot wide. I was unaware of the potential size of this plant; I bought it on a whim because I was drawn to its unusual leaves. As I wandered my garden trying to figure out where to plant it, I luckily came upon a wide-open spot and imagined it would shine here. It has, for many years now. In your garden, surround this plant with many low flowers, so that it really stands out, or place it in a perennial border, preferably toward the front, so that visitors can instantly see its effusive foliage.

Totally opposite in scale from this crambe is *Phuopsis stylosa*. It grows in sun or light shade and requires average moisture. This multipurpose but little-known groundcover resembles clusters of pincushions massed together. The medium-pink, starry flowers look much like pins as they sit above their green carpet in early spring, and then go on to provide four months of color. An unusual aspect of this plant is its characteristic pungent scent. Pungent is putting it mildly, since some people say it smells like a skunk! To avoid offending anyone, I didn't plant it near any doors to my house. Far back in my garden, it forms spreading patches under *Crataegus ambigua* (Russian hawthorn)—but it is still located near a path so visitors can ask what the strange odor is!

Iris leaves and the deep-cupped blooms of *Tulipa kaufmanniana* 'Ancilla' break through
the gray dissected foliage of Artemisia 'Valerie Finnis' (white sage).

Another plant for all diehard foliage lovers to lust after is *Rhodiola arctica*. This sedum relative, which I casually bought at a plant sale, sits near a large rock not far from my patio. It forms a circular medallion that in spring, like a cake in the oven, gently rises to about six inches high and as wide. Its tiny nubs appear red at first, and then the intricate, succulent gray-green stems grow and look like a miniature accordion. The top of the plant has an attractive dark red rosette, which has charm from spring until frost.

Like the waves of the ocean, my garden is continually changing. No matter what the season, something fabulous is always on the horizon. The wheels are always churning in my psyche as I cheerfully step out into my garden ready to see what magical pictures I can conjure. As the artist, I must satisfy my longing for visual excellence in harmony and grandeur. I often never know what will hit the mark artistically for me. I don't purchase plants only by height or color or texture, but through a combination of all these aspects and how I feel internally at the moment.

A pretty spring/summer collage occurs when I unite plants and stones that have contrasting textures and colors, stretching the seasons. In spring, the versatile hardy ground-

The bluish-green texture of *Rhodiola arctica* (sedum) on the left complements the red flowers of *Helianthemum red* (sunrose), both of which play off the stone trough and large smooth rock.

Photograph by John Davenport

cover *Delosperma nubigenum* (yellow ice plant) is ablaze with small, bright yellow flowers. When it finishes blooming in June, the sheet of plump bright green nubs looks pleasing as it sneaks onto my red flagstone path. Growing close to this path is *Thymus pseudolanuginosus* (woolly thyme). This popular and familiar groundcover has low, fuzzy, silvery-gray foliage that marches over walks and walls. The fragrant lavender summer flowers add to its appeal; in winter it offers a purplish cast.

I mentioned *Crambe cordifolia* a few paragraphs back. *Crambe maritima* (sea kale) is also an excellent foliage plant. A member of the mustard family, and related to such vegetables as cabbage and broccoli, it is smaller than *C. cordifolia*, and an exuberant addition to the perennial border. Its beautiful large, glaucous leaves have thick blades that are exquisitely curved and lobed. Natural rainfall or water from a sprinkler (which it doesn't need much of) leaves clear sparkling droplets dancing on the leaves. During the searing heat of summer, small white flowers emerge, augmenting the splendor of this plant. With its compact size (under two feet), wavy texture, and gray-green foliage, *C. maritima* would look lovely near the front of any border, or with its leaves falling near a red flagstone patio, which is where I have mine planted. Other plants that look excellent with this crambe are *Helictotrichon semper-virens* (blue oat grass or blue avena grass) and *Iris pallida* 'Variegata', with its narrow lines and variegated foliage.

For more foliage interest practically year round, I adore table mountain ice plant (*Delosperma* 'John Proffitt'). This succulent groundcover, with its rich green and red leaves, persists into winter. From May through July it is smothered with one-inch daisylike, hot-pink flowers. I even see it bloom sporadically August through October and into November, if we have not been smacked with a major snowstorm. I followed a hunch and planted it along one of my sunny paths, a location where it has been satisfied. It also makes a grand slam in another area: On a short, steep berm, where I painstakingly shoved in a medium-size granite boulder, this ice plant is tightly packed against the stone, slowly crawling up and down the slope. It has gradually spread out over two feet. For next year I have a brilliant idea—I'm going to attempt to carefully plant some bulbs of *Tulipa batalinii* in with this groundcover, so that they will bloom first and, after their foliage dies back, table mountain ice plant will continue the showy blooming cycle.

In this same sunny area, but on the other side of the rock-covered hill, is *Ruschia putterillii*, an import from a South African plant expedition. This twelve-inch-high, firm-textured evergreen shrublet spreads to three feet and firmly hugs the ground. It adapts well to low-water sites, and shows eye-catching pink pinwheel flowers in spring. Its long, thin, succulent branches create many curves as they twist all about. A child might have fun looking into this dense shrub, as well as touching its firm stems and poking fingers into the holes. Along the bluish-green and red branches is intricate foliage that looks like tiny protruding nubs. The many choices for companion plants include clump-forming short grasses, which help soften the stiff appearance of the ruschia. Pairing it up with the silvery, soft gray leaves of various artemisias is also nice; try *Artemisia pycnocephala* 'David's Choice' or, if you prefer larger leaflets, use the spreading cushion form of *A. stelleriana* named 'Silver Brocade'.

On a nearby low embankment is the shrubby semi-evergreen *Lotus hirsutus* (canary clover). This ten-inch pillowlike plant has gray-green, velvet-soft branches that gently bend over each other. The pea-sized flowers, white tinged with pink, appear for several weeks in summer. They are succeeded by reddish brown seedpods, which glimmer like tiny pieces of coffee-colored hard candy that you just might want to nibble! A nice companion plant, and one that adds more silver to the picture, is the larger shrub *Caryopteris* x *clandonensis* (blue mist spirea).

As a background plant, and to point up the silvery hues, ornamental grasses are again good companions. In this instance, I surmised that a small specimen would not do; the planting needed a larger form. With dense, linear foliage and an open vase habit, *Pennisetum alopecuroides* 'Moudry' (fountain grass) is an excellent choice. Not including its dark purple-black flowers, it grows two feet high and four feet wide. As Rick Darke notes in *The Color Encyclopedia of Ornamental Grasses*—and my experience agrees with this—sometimes this variety does not produce flowers. Curious about its behavior, I inspected the plant thoroughly. Lo and behold, when I teased back the long, wide leaves I uncovered two-inch inflorescences that looked as though they were just itching to emerge! They didn't make it before the snow came, but in my opinion, although these dark-colored plumes are spectacular, they are not essential to the beauty and usefulness of this plant. (Besides, this grass, once its seeds ripen and scatter, can aggressively seed itself around, especially if it gets extra moisture.) The golden-yellow autumn color of the leaves is lustrous, and it remains, making the plant resemble a big mushroom through winter and into spring. This special grass needs more publicity to reach the many homeowners who would appreciate its potential in their gardens.

More Foliage

The group of plants called euphorbias (spurges) contains many excellent perennials that lend a spark to sunny spots. The genus *Euphorbia* boasts over two thousand species. Most are subtropical or tropical, hailing from South Africa, Egypt, and Thailand, but a dozen or so come from places such as the Himalayas and thus can tolerate subzero temperatures. I love knowing the original homes of some of the plants in my garden. I imagine plant explorers traipsing the globe for beautiful specimens. Voilà! Once they have been discovered, these plants arrive in my backyard without any travel (or much cost) on my part, giving my garden an international flair.

In Colorado and other locations in the Rocky Mountain West, euphorbias thrive. Some like a dry location, while others, such as *E. palustris*, perform well with additional moisture. I have been growing *E. palustris* for a few years. In spring, its bold and brilliant lime-green foliage, with touches of deep yellow and burgundy, brings new radiance to the garden. It grows four feet in height as well as in width. The euphorbia is located at the bottom of a minimal incline where water trickles down from a higher spot, providing the added moisture that it prefers. Its foliage blends easily with the bolder coloring of roses. As a backdrop I have planted the double pink rose 'Applejack'. However, even before the rose bursts into bloom, this rather quiet foliage plant can create a cohesive spring picture when surrounded with other perennials. *Helictotrichon sempervirens* (blue oat grass or blue avena grass), with its blue spikes, is a great choice, as is any tall yellow or double frilly white daffodil; the yellow one would pick up on the yellow coloring in the euphorbia. Across a narrow path, not far from the euphorbia but in a dryer spot, I have clumps of the lacy, low *Veronica armena* (Armenian speedwell), which produces its tiny sky-blue flowers for almost a month in early spring.

Euphorbias are well praised in garden literature. The much-admired horticulturist Graham Stuart Thomas uses such words as "handsome," "invaluable," and "superior." In most cases, I wholeheartedly agree with his assessments—except of course for aggressive performers such as *E. cyparissias* (cypress spurge), with its feathery foliage and yellow-green bracts, and *E. myrsinites* (donkey-tail spurge), with its familiar blue-green florets and wavy stems. I never purchased this last species, but it snuck into my garden anyhow, probably from a neighbor's yard. It has trailing blue-green stems and in early spring is covered with lime-

Marrubium rotundifolium (horehound) gives texture galore,
especially when punctuated by **Muscari armeniacum** 'Blue Spike' (grape hyacinth).

Luminous granite stone and the circle daisies of Delosperma 'John Proffitt' (table mountain ice plant) make a perfect combination.

yellow bracts. It is not a personal favorite of mine, probably because—and I humbly admit to a touch of snobbery—it is too ordinary and also because it pops up all over and, in my opinion, is quite weedy. I'm always snatching it out wherever I see its foliage sneaking in.

Despite these few weedy forms, many gardeners find euphorbias to be a tremendous asset in the landscape. With their captivating foliage (reddish stems and chartreuse bracts), they are winners throughout the growing season. *E. dulcis* 'Chameleon' is a striking form about a foot tall, with hues of aubergine, brown, and green. In spring this rare coloration is a delight to see, especially combined with the many varieties of perky yellow dwarf daffodils: Try 'Topolino', which is creamy yellow changing to ivory, as well as *Narcissus bulbocodium* var. *conspicuus* (hoop petticoat daffodil), a native of Spain and Portugal, with golden yellow, funnel-shaped flowers and grasslike foliage.

A better-known euphorbia is *E. polychroma*. It is low and dome shaped, about a foot high, with yellow bracts. It performs best without abundant moisture. Place a few of these spurges together, and surround them with *Muscari armeniacum* 'Blue Spike' (grape hyacinth). The yellow bracts and the blue flowers are a perfect pairing. This double form of grape hyacinth is larger and bushier than the species. Or try *M. latifolium*, a two-toned form with top florets of light blue and bottom ones of a deep violet. These so-called minor bulbs are inexpensive at nurseries and through mail-order catalogs. Be generous with yourself; you will be glad you did when they sweep across your landscape in spring.

Another foliage winner for the dry or barely watered garden is *Marrubium rotundifolium* (horehound). This low-growing herb is under ten inches, but with the addition of the tiered purple flowers its height is almost fifteen inches. Once the flowering cycle has finished, the disk-shaped brown seedheads can be cut off or left on, depending on your wishes and your level of tidiness. At this stage what remains is a light green, slightly silvery, textured ground-cover, with each dime-sized soft leaf etched in white. Because I crave the sparkle silver brings to my garden, I have let this plant romp easily over my low walls as it penetrates into the middle of my various rock formations.

For a smart look in one section of my garden, I have haphazardly mixed the poppy *Papaver dubium* in with the marrubium. It has quarter-sized red blooms and appears to dance in front of the purple flowers of the horehound. Also nearby are various festucas, which add blue tones and vertical interest.

High and Dry

In the strict sense, to be "high and dry" means that you are out of luck, stuck, stranded, and without water! From the Western gardener's perspective, the opposite is in fact true. Here in the Rocky Mountain region we are quite fortunate, with abundant sunshine, low moisture, and great growing conditions. Although we are not literally out of water, conserving our natural resources is an ecologically aware thing to do. If we grow dryland plants, we can also keep watering to a minimum. Surrounded by the Rockies, we are naturally high, so in an informal manner the phrase "high and dry" fits us perfectly.

Whether we are high in the mountains or at sea level, as gardeners, we are prone to get a bit heavy-handed with the amount of water we pour onto our precious plants. We mistakenly believe that if a plant is not performing up to par, or if it is looking poorly, it must need more water. If we control our tendency to overwater, we can grow a host of plants successfully. Many low-water plants have appealing geometrical habits and equally appealing tones of gray. Although in general they are well adapted to dry conditions, sometimes, especially when temperatures inch up to the nineties or hundreds for prolonged stretches of time, I do monitor their needs and water them when necessary.

A plant that never needs any extra water is *Yucca baccata* (banana yucca). After growing it for a number of years, I know I will soon see the white clusters of flowers it is known for. I surmise that this delay is because I initially planted it from a very small pot and the plant has not yet reached flowering potential. The lightish green, swordlike spikes from which the flower emerges become narrow and quite sharp toward the tips. It grows to two feet high, with a spread of three feet. Each two-inch-thick spike, which curves slightly inward, is dressed with hair-thin curls scattered on its edges. This evergreen Western native is conspicuously placed near a smooth red-and-black rectangular boulder along a path, but not so close as to jab people walking by! Next to the yucca and also caressing the rock is a shrub named rabbitbrush (*Chrysothamnus nauseosus*). Its silver leaves and yellow flowers add softness to the scene when fall is in its glory; even in the dark winter days of February its whitish gray-green stems offer color and form for the gardener to admire as spring seems far off on the horizon.

Also adjacent to this area is *Ephedra nevadensis* (Mormon tea). This four-by-four-foot globular shrub has thin, flexible stems that are coarsely textured and similar in appearance to bamboo. Excellent for a xeriscape, it also is not bothered by a little extra moisture. I purchased it when it was small and shoved it between boulders; now it looks quite content stuffed in there. Because of its size, no matter the season, this shrub dominates the site. Last year, in late summer, I was delighted when the red berries it is known for finally appeared; these give gardeners another wonderful reason to purchase this shrub.

Circling the ephedra and the yucca are clumps of *Armeria maritima* 'Rubrifolia' (sea pink or thrift), looking much like the tops of ice cream cones that have melted together. Mass many of these together, and a wave of burgundy foliage will be at your feet as you stroll through your garden. In spring, the foliage is topped with small, round, pink flowers on short, thin stems.

I have planted *Ephedra equisetine* on my south side garden bed, where there is little moisture and the sun rages throughout the season. Here, on a raised berm, it stands out as an aristocrat among a flurry of other perennials. Below the shrub is the familiar and easy evergreen groundcover *Iberis sempervirens* (candytuft), with its spring cover of white flowers. Flowering about the same time as the candytuft is *Veronica peduncularis* 'Georgia Blue'. The bushy, spreading foliage is semi-evergreen and grows to six inches, with loads of tiny, cupped, deep blue flowers. Also in this area is *Hieracium lanatum* (hawkweed). Unlike some of its aggressive relatives, this eight-inch-high plant is slow to spread. It has woolly, felted, gray-green, three-inch leaves, which appear tailor-made to lie flat on the surrounding gravel. Rising above the hairy foliage are stems topped with yellow, dandelion-like flowers, flashy as they emerge from the silvery leaves. Blooming here too is *Dianthus knappii* (garden pink). Endemic to Western Yugoslavia, this sulphur-yellow dianthus is loosely branched and stands about a foot high, with flowers clustered close together. I like growing this particular variety because it is the only yellow dianthus among three hundred different species.

A definite favorite of mine, but one that wants an occasional sip of water, is *Othonna capensis* (Little-pickles). The name alone was enough to evoke my curiosity, so I bought it instantly. It has come into the trade thanks to an expedition that Panayoti Kelaidis made to the Drakenburg mountain range of South Africa. Since it comes from a mountainous region, it performs well at elevations up to eight thousand feet. A mat-forming plant that can eventually spread to twelve inches, it has pudgy, blue-green "pickle-shaped" foliage. It blooms on short stems, with small, button-shaped yellow daisies. Before they open, the pearl-sized flower buds are touched with tints of mauve, which adds to the plant's attractiveness. One of the longest-flowering plants in my garden, it begins blooming in April or May and keeps puffing along into November, undaunted by chilly weather and occasional snow. On a warm, sunlit fall day, leaves from my cottonwood swirl about it as yellow-and-black bees huddle around it, searching the flowers for hints of pollen that summer has left behind. An excellent companion plant is *Origanum laevigatum* 'Hopley's'. It has fine-textured leaves and delicate lavender flowers. Close to a foot tall, it blooms from late summer into fall. In spring the matted groundcover *Veronica liwanensis* (Turkish veronica), with its iridescent blue flowers, complements Little-pickles and its sunny round flowers.

Adding a bit of sparkle to this south side garden and combining well with all the yellows and the silver-foliaged plants is *Penstemon eatonii* (Eaton's firecracker). This two-and-a-half-foot penstemon, with its dark green, pointed, leathery leaves may be short lived, but it

Eriogonum subalpinum (buckwheat) takes center stage with
Papaver trinifolium (Armenian poppy) on the right.

The yellow seedhead of *Eriogonum umbellatum* (buckwheat) in the lower left corner creates a nice juxtaposition with the blue flowers of *Lallemantia canescens* on the right. The other blue Penstemon on the left stands out well when mixed with the stone and the pink flowers above of *Salvia recognita*.

freely seeds around the garden. The foliage is usually evergreen with red markings. Its bright red tubular flowers appear in May and are delightful. Each clump may produce as many as ten of these elegant flowering stems.

For a contrasting look, near the penstemon is the summer-blooming shrub *Chamaebatiaria millefolium* (fernbush). The white aromatic flowers are slightly pyramidal and appear on the tips of the ferny gray-green foliage. This shrub usually grows three feet high and wide, but it is variable, sometimes reaching five or six feet. At its base I have used *Dianthus nardiformis* (cloud pink), which displays nickel-sized fragrant flowers in a marvelous shade of lavender-pink; it also offers wispy foliage laid out like a small compact pillow. A wonderful ornamental oregano to plant with the dianthus, around the fern bush, is *Origanum laevigatum* 'Herrenhausen'. In summer the small flowers are dark purple with flecks of pale lavender. Through many winters the foliage of the fernbush remains gray-green, and the brown, slightly curved branches inject artistry into the winter landscape.

A flower that definitely fits in the "high and dry" category is the biennial *Berlandiera lyrata*, more deliciously known as "the chocolate flower." On a warm, sun-filled spring day the scent of milk chocolate wafts through the air, as if a Hershey's-like flavor were touching one's lips and tongue. At the Denver Botanic Gardens this ten-inch yellow daisy is planted near a path. Children walking past can inhale it, enjoying the yummy fragrance and begging their parents to buy them a chocolate bar. This plant may cause more hassles than parents bargained for on a simple jaunt to their local botanic garden!

All these artistic plant portraits appearing in unison are supported by my basic underlying theme of intuition and imagination. These two ideas offer the firm foundation as I experiment and wonder where each plant might look its best. Although this approach may seem, to the outside observer, carefree to the point of haphazardness, it is backed up by a lot of thought and knowledge about plants and how they behave in the garden. When I had my business, I would gather a hundred or so plants that I had purchased at the nursery and bring them to the client's house. I would group the varieties together in the flower bed I was working on, along with special specimens that had appealed to me or that the client wanted. Then I would move slowly about among the plants, reflecting on placement, spacing, color, and other design ideas that I had learned over the years, *remembering that plants can always be moved*. This task required a combination of arranging puzzle parts so that they "clicked" together and bringing in the artistic flow that came from an internal sense.

I use this exact approach for my own garden, whether I am preparing a large bed or just planting five or ten plants. Regardless of the scope of a project, I give careful attention to what feels and looks best. Sometimes I change my mind often; at other times I quickly feel the right arrangement as I move black containers from one spot to another, imagining how the mature plants will look down the road.

For myself, as an intuitive gardener, it is far too confusing if I think too much about height, color, spacing, bloom size, and season of bloom, so I usually focus on color and height and let the other elements weave themselves in naturally. Sometimes, as I install the plants, I leave an opening for something special to be planted later, or I return to the nursery looking for just the right plant for a spot. So I always try to stay with my intuitive sense, hoping that my choices will result in a concert of color, texture, and shape.

Eriogonums and Pulsatillas

Two groups of plants come to mind when I reflect on long-term animation and texture in the sunny garden. One is the eriogonums (buckwheats), and the other is the pulsatillas (pasque flowers). First I will explore the eriogonums. Whether your garden is large or small, these gems will add diversity to your landscape, blooming from May through early fall. The genus *Eriogonum* comprises over two hundred species, including annuals, perennials, and subshrubs. Because many are native to the arid regions of the western United States, they adapt superbly to Western gardens. In the wild, they range from the plains and deserts to the alpine peaks. The mountain habitat is their natural home, so, depending on your site, you may need to add gravel to the soil. All of them require good drainage and somewhat dry conditions, although I have found that *E. umbellatum* and *E. subalpinum* can tolerate slight amounts of extra moisture and do well. This is probably because plants at the higher elevations receive more moisture, yet they face harsh climatic conditions—snow and strong winds—in both summer and winter. (A good source of further information on the geography and climate of our region is *Rocky Mountain Alpines*, edited by Jean Williams.) If you can, learn the natural habitat of any plant you purchase and try to mimic that in your home garden. If you accidentally give eriogonums more moisture than they want and they go to plant heaven, recall the motto I've learned over the years and live by in my garden: "Replace it fast!"

Until recently, buckwheats were the province of discriminating rock gardeners. Knowledgeable gardeners craved these choice plants, often going down on their hands and knees to inspect and admire them. Now, as gardening is enjoying a renaissance, offering relaxation and relief in our fast-paced, computer-driven culture, some of these special garden plants are more available. While seed collectors and plant explorers comb mountain ranges seeking out new selections to offer connoisseurs, in some areas you may still have to ask your garden center to order buckwheats.

There is a great deal of variation in this complex genus. Two low ones I grow are *E. jamesii* and *E. subalpinum*. The first grows to twelve inches high, with gray-green (often evergreen) leaves that look like tiny teaspoons. The flowers of my plants are yellow, but in the wild they can be white or cream. The second one, about the same height, sits near the top of one of my

The vibrant colors of the orangey *Helianthemum nummularium* 'Ben Nevis' (sunrose), the bright pink Dianthus (pinks), and the tubular *Penstemon alamoensis* (beard tongue) all mingle well when complemented by the linear lines of *Iris lactea* and the frilly foliage of *Papaver somniferum* (opium poppy).

rock gardens and has flat-topped umbels of pale yellow flowers. It has small, gray-green leaves that turn rusty red in fall. Over time this plant forms a dense mat.

Two larger forms that I'm pleased to grow are *E. corymbosum* and *E. niveum*. I've grown these two for only a few years, but I have seen mature specimens, and their frothy appearance in fall and winter is breathtaking. *E. corymbosum* reaches two and a half feet high and over four feet wide. It has wire-thin stems that rebranch a few times, as a tree does. Flower color on this dome-shaped plant is buff, but in fall the blooms often turn shades of rose pink. *E. niveum*, with white flowers, will be shorter about eighteen to twenty-four inches high, but still can reach four feet in width.

These buckwheats would not do well placed at the edge of a lush perennial border, where they would definitely get too much water. Nor, in my opinion, would they look appropriate; from an intuitive and aesthetic point of view, they would not blend well together. Planting them there would be like planting a rhododendron in a cactus garden! Instead, reserve a space for them in a rock garden, in a trough, or along a rock wall, where they will accent the massive stone. A dry mound or simple slope with full-sun exposure would also be an ideal spot. If you plant them near paths, you can have the pleasure of closely observing their changing leaf color.

One eriogonum that has been a constant near the bottom of one of my rock gardens is *E. umbellatum* (sulfur flower). A slow and steady grower, it blooms from late spring into summer with lemon-yellow flowers that pop up to ten inches. As the blooms fade in late

The color and textures of the four-petalled *Oenothera acaulis* (evening primrose), the cushiony and tight *Picea abies* 'Little Gem' (spruce), and the *Helianthemum red* (sunrose) create a harmonious scene.

summer, the flower still looks attractive, with hints of pale yellow and shades of tan. Beneath the lollipop-like flowers is a mat of evergreen leaves whose undersides are textured woolly white. In fall the foliage turns russet or sometimes shades of purple; it persists through winter and is a delight on dreary, cool days. In my gravelly and lightly amended soil, my patch has spread to four feet. This is a long-lived plant whose needs are minimal. It can even tolerate some shade, and it is undaunted by winter winds or snow cover.

Above this groundcover I have used various penstemons. They add height and bright color to the scene, and their tonguelike flowers are mesmerizing. Sometimes I like the gentler hues of violet and soft pink, but often, possibly because of my extroverted nature, I am drawn to varieties in trumpet-loud shades of red, such as *Penstemon barbatus*, with its slightly curving long stem and thin, tubular red flowers. Other red choices are *P. cardinalis*, a species that reaches over two feet high, and, for larger, dark reddish purple flowers, *P. 'Garnet'*.

Among the low eriogonums and the tall penstemons I have planted *Teucrium aroanium* (Styx germander), an easy lavender groundcover that fills in any bare spots. In this area is also a nicely shaped dwarf conifer with many short and irregular branches. Together with *Eriogonum umbellatum*, these two radically different plants, both highly textured, create a feast for the eyes from December until April. They appear harmonious and almost Christmasy with their red and green colors. The red and gray boulders nearby help illuminate the green needles and vice versa.

All of these contrasts—tall evergreens, mat-forming groundcovers, and solid masses of stone—illustrate how the theme of intuition and imagination drifts throughout my garden. Obviously, I buy my plants because I adore their color, shape, or texture, but I place them in my garden where I imagine they will be the most showy, will highlight specific spots, or will create quiet harmonies. To reach a decision I focus simultaneously on what is simmering in my psyche and on the outer needs in the garden. Gardening nicely concretizes the philosophical side of heady concepts. Where to put a tall plant? Where would a groundcover serve the garden best? One can use both rational and intuitive guidelines to answer such questions. Logically, tall plants are great at the back of any border, but they also are visual exclamation points when sited near the edge of the garden or close to a path. Groundcovers are great for mass appeal, so, depending on the size of your garden, give them a few feet of space.

As I mentioned in Chapter One, structural plants such as evergreens, trees, and shrubs give grounding and create the "bones" of the garden. Often these structural elements are placed around the edges of the garden, but again, scattering one or two in the middle or to the side of any kind of mass planting catches garden visitors off guard and grabs their attention. Once all these features collectively meld, the beauty of the garden is increased.

Of special importance is that the gardener bring in his or her own personality, just as people do when designing the inside of a home. As gardeners create gardens, they discover their own likes and dislikes, and they need to follow that creative energy.

Pulsatillas (pasque flowers) also provide more than one season of interest in the garden. They are one of the earliest flowers to bloom in spring, and later, in summer, their seedheads are bouncy-looking whorls. Their habitat is widespread, ranging from the Great Plains and woodland areas and stretching upwards to 12,000 feet. One of the species, *Pulsatilla patens*, is the state flower of South Dakota. In most years, in the wild, it is possible to find the pasque flower blooming from March into July. I have fond memories of admiring *P. vulgaris*, the common European species, when I volunteered at the Denver Botanic Gardens Rock Alpine Garden. "How can I get this flower to look so beautiful in my garden?" I quizzed Panayoti. "Just scatter some seed," he said simply. So, one spring day, after a volunteer group had collected a plentiful amount of seed, I rushed home and, with no specific pattern in mind, tossed seeds into my newly made rock garden. Like an excited child, I anticipated abundant bloom. The following spring I had a few sparkling dabs of purple, but over the years, colorful colonies of *P. vulgaris* have successfully multiplied. They were so successful that, ten years later, I have been forced to eliminate a few clumps here and there to make room for other choice plants.

As wonderful as all the other seasons are, almost nothing can compare to the desire and craving for spring, when that first bud or green shoot emerges, a trigger for oodles of future blooms. In late winter one year, while I was topdressing my garden with a load of lush screened cow manure, I began to tidy up a bit. I was delighted to notice the fuzzy, silvery, soft nubs of the pulsatilla peeking out from beneath last year's dilapidated brown foliage. The pasque flower is almost oblivious to snow and shivering cold weather; in fact, it enjoys the cool temperatures of late winter and early spring. Once it has bloomed, I know spring has finally arrived. No matter how many times I see this same flower, the thrill always returns. During spring, my emotions are in high gear as my eyes collide with various flowers that take off and begin their blooming cycle. I look at areas that need extra plants here or there, which gives me the chance to dash off to the nursery to fuel my passion. I also feel an internal rush for the next flower to bloom. I'm excited to see plants fill in and mature. Plants that were small a year ago are now bigger, more colorful and robust.

Each pulsatilla has one or several stems, each crowned by a large, solitary flower. Their showy blooms are deep, cuplike shapes in various shades of purple and white, dabbed with yellow centers. Some forms are burgundy-red, and there is an unusual yellow one that I cherish. (The yellow look-alike is not actually a pulsatilla, but *Anemone mulifida* 'Magellanica', probably from South America, and closely related to the pulsatillas.) These spectacular flowers beckon onlookers to glance down and flirt with their beauty. At six inches their shades of purple mingle among the red and tan pea gravel that carpets my rock garden.

For many years I have wanted to scatter dwarf yellow daffodils among the purple flowers, but alas, that chore has never been done. In the years when I was planting hundreds of bulbs for clients, sometimes my energy petered out for my garden! So I highly recommend it to you, my reader. Think of the look: a sea of purple flowers with yellow centers, and in the midst of them, projecting through the earth, ten-inch-high, trumpeted dwarf daffodils. These two plants demonstrate how the intuitive process works in one's mind or in the garden, uniting two diverse plants that bloom in unison to create an effusive spectacle.

A strong trademark of the pulsatillas is their ornamental, fuzzy seedheads, which appear in late spring once the flower has finished blooming. They have a golden tint and look light as a feather, as though they would blow off in the wind. The common name "windflower," usually applied to anemones, is sometimes used to refer to this plant, since the wind helps disperse its seeds. The charming seedheads remain on the plant well into the summer season, adding an iridescent glimmer to the garden, by themselves and also when other plants arrive on the scene.

For passionate gardeners and those who desire something that no one in their neighborhood is likely to have, the eriogonums and pulsatillas are great pluses in a garden of any size, providing waves of appeal for many months.

Sassy Summer Seedheads

Once a flower has completed its blooming cycle, the seedhead that remains contributes an essential feature in the makeup of my garden. The texture, shape, color, and height of different seedheads mingle with structural elements and with other plants. While wandering my garden late one summer evening, after the sun had set, I was drawn to an unlikely combination: peonies and alliums. Both had long since finished blooming, and I had cut off the ratty flowers of the peonies. (Not all seedheads are to be admired.) I was left with neat green pointed foliage, which lingers well into fall, when the leaves may turn shades of red and bronze. The globe-shaped skeletal remains of the *Allium schubertii* flowerhead looked like a spaceship that had settled in from outer space. Others have compared its appearance to a burst of fireworks. This particular allium, native to the Mediterranean region and North Africa, is one of the most unusual ornamental onions I have come across. The globular umbels, which appear on stems one to two feet high in early summer, are pale lavender or

The lettered flat "DREAM" stone adds the finishing touch when knitted together with the linear lines of *Festuca* sp. (fescue) and the silvery-gray leaves of *Tanacetum densum* var. *amani* (partridge feather). *Anemone multifida*, topped with cottony puffs, and *Asclepias tuberosa* (butterfly weed) complete the composition.

light pink. Each umbel can be up to ten inches across, and the pedicels (the individual stalks that make up the umbel) extend outward in varying lengths. At summer's end, its framework is still visually dramatic. At the tips of the thin beige pedicels are round tiny balls (seed capsules) shaded light olive green. In fall, one can clearly see the charcoal-black seeds tucked within the capsule. The foliage of the peony looks thick, lush, and rich. The marriage of these two diametrically opposed plants gives rise to an exquisite work of art. Surrounding both of these plants is a carpet of *Fragaria* 'Pink Panda'. This strawberry produces small, sweet red berries, along with dainty pink flowers that bloom spring into fall. It's fun to reach down for a yummy snack as I weed my garden!

One trouble-free plant that has given me years of pleasure as it billows over rocks and pebbles is *Santolina chamaecyparissus* (lavender cotton). This drought-tolerant, highly textured silver plant grows to about a foot. In early summer yellow flowers emerge. As summer heats up and moves along, the yellow color fades, leaving behind a sea of tan, green, and dimming yellow pea-sized seedheads. In my extemporaneous approach to gardening, I rarely shear the old blooms off this large (four feet across) plant because I like the brownish yellow seedheads. I would rather direct my attention to general weeding or putting in new plants than tediously trimming off old blooms. In this instance I am willing to sacrifice a few more flowers. (In other situations, as with a small dianthus, I may choose to trim off the finished blooms because I want to enjoy another flush of color.)

For dry conditions near smooth stone, I have a favorite arrangement of plants with distinct characteristics. Trusting my good intuition, I try to create a balance between the stones and plants as they draw energy from each other, creating a magical garden moment. A good friend who knew of my love of gardening and Jungian psychology gave me a flat rock with the word "DREAM" carved into it. This unique solid presence adds curiosity and appeal, especially situated next to complementary plants. Stones, rocks, or practically any hardscape element, when used constructively and gently, will add contrast to the picture. All of my other rocks either look rugged, with jagged edges, or are small stones the size of peas. This one stands out because of its different texture and the large carved word "DREAM". Close to this smooth rock is a mat of silvery *Tanacetum densum* subsp. *amani* (partridge feather), which looks like an intricately decorated piece of carpet. It lies flat against my "DREAM" rock, sweeping over a corner of it. The second plant I use is *Anemone multifida*, whose seedheads resemble small, puffy, white cotton candy on a stick. The third plant is *Asclepias tuberosa* (butterfly weed), which begins to bloom in July with attractive orange flowers that butterflies love. Completing this late-summer artistic scene are the slender blades of *Festuca glauca* (blue fescue).

For summer seedheads, I like *Penstemon strictus* (Rocky Mountain penstemon). An easy-care plant, this Western native adapts to a wide range of conditions. It's not fussy — a little more moisture or a bit less doesn't disturb it. After the lavender/blue flowers finish blooming in midsummer, I leave the seedheads alone. When they are still unripened, the reddish purple spiky capsules almost look like tiny grapes running up and down the stalk. As I do with many other plants in my garden, I let this one self-seed, so in late spring I see its carefree blooms throughout my garden. At two feet, this penstemon is dwarfed by the bushy *Cephalaria gigantea* (Tatarian cephalaria), which reaches six feet high. Its cushionlike flower explodes in early summer at the back of my perennial and shrub border. The puffy, half-dollar-sized, pale yellow flowers appear three feet above the large, highly toothed, pointed green leaves. When the flower finishes, my landscape is heavily dotted with light green, black-flecked round seedheads. This plant generously seeds around, so in late summer I do my best to remember to snip many of the dried seedheads off to rein in its behavior.

A most statuesque perennial with a distinctive seedhead is *Kitaibela vitifolia* (Russian hibiscus). Many gardeners instantly recognize its pointed, lobed leaves and know correctly that it is related to the old-fashioned hollyhock. Russian hibiscus is a hard plant to find; I came across it at a local specialty nursery a few years ago. Hardy to near twenty below zero, it offers half-inch cup-shaped flowers in shades of pink and white from summer into fall. The blooms face skyward, which may be why some gardeners seldom plant this flower in their borders. Mine is planted adjacent to a grass path, where it is visible as I stroll by. In mid- to late summer, as the blooms finish, the semi-round shells first turn chartreuse, and shortly after change again and become dark brown and hairy, standing out in the landscape. Nearby I have the three-foot grass *Calamagrostis brachytricha* (Korean feather reed grass). With its densely tufted, narrow green foliage, it bonds with the brown capsules and the maple-shaped leaves of the *Kitaibela*. A fragrant, double red shrub rose blooms in the area, as well as *Eryngium planum* (sea holly). As fall pushes summer into the past, the eryngium turns tan, and its prickly, long-lasting flowerheads offer an excellent choice for dried flower arrangements.

Another eryngium with an admirable seedhead is *E. yuccifolium*. A North American native first described in 1699, this sea holly is not spectacular, but it is definitely worth planting if you are searching for the unusual. Its specific epithet aptly describes its foliage, which is similar to the yucca plant, although much softer. Like the yucca, it has small, wispy hairs adorning its blue-gray leaves. Rising out of the long, limp foliage is a two-foot stalk crowned with a spiny, round, pale green floret. Alone, this pale seedhead is not commanding in the garden, but it can be creatively incorporated to highlight and mix well with other plants. For instance, I intermingle mine with the long-stemmed annual *Verbena bonariensis*. The flowers of the two plants are similar in size and shape, but the verbena has lavender flowers. Lavender and light green play off each other nicely. The stems of both plants are also similar; placed near one another, with all their unusual parts, these plants create a sparkling floral picture.

Seedheads of various plants add an element of flair to the garden that many gardeners may not at first notice or think about. As I fell more and more in love with gardening, I became aware of these distinctive attributes. From my viewpoint, the beauty of some seedheads is comparable to the beauty of the flower. I particularly love clematis for its wide color range—apricots, various reds, pinks, and shades of purple and blue. But I am also enamored of its small, silvery, moppy-looking seedheads. Try any clematis color to your liking with the single red rose 'Dortmund'. The relationship between these two plants is heightened when the clematis is finished blooming and the seedheads seem to glow next to the hollylike shine of the rose foliage. When you are plant shopping, go for tons of color and texture, but to add chic to your garden, now and then look for plants that will be tempting to the eye after the bloom has finished.

Dwarf Conifers

Dwarf conifers are specimens that are smaller than related members of that family. But don't be fooled—"dwarf" does not always mean "small." A conifer labeled "dwarf" may grow too large for a particular site, so check out your sources well before purchasing. Many of us know what can happen otherwise. We have seen it all too often in our neighborhoods. The pine tree planted three feet from the driveway now towers over the yard. I see many blue spruce trees that have been chopped and sheared, leaving behind ragged brown stems. People are drawn to buy these cute spruces at our local grocery store, not having the faintest idea that, over time, they may reach forty to sixty feet. By that time, the homeowner may have moved and the tree has become someone else's problem. Or twenty years down the road, because of improper pruning techniques, the specimen needs to be ripped out.

If they do fit the site, however, these expensive dwarf specimens add a special exuberance to the design of the garden. I have distributed a few of these characters around my garden because I like their profiles, color, and evergreen characteristics. (And nothing gets coddled in my garden. These plants need to be rugged to withstand the strong winds, winter sun, and various elements that the Colorado climate has to offer.)

In recent years there have been many books written about how powerful structure can be in the garden. It's useful to remember that structure can come from non-hardscape elements; these conifers bring in bulk that helps shape the garden. As they mature, they act as living sculptures that add height, diversity, and color. Their visibility in winter is a tremendous asset to the appeal of the garden as they mingle and play off other garden features such as smooth flagstone, pebbles, colored boulders, and wooden fences. I let my intuitive sense of design come in as I imagine where to harmoniously place these evergreens. I may gaze at an area for a while, until an inner lightbulb comes on and I know just where to plant one of these conifers. I particularly like them located at the bottom of hills, just where one may not anticipate them to be, since mostly low plants may be planted there. Because of their strongly green foliage, no matter what its texture, they are superb placed near any large rock, preferably one that is richly patterned with color and blotches. They are the bones of the garden, occupying space and helping to ground and solidify the entire picture.

In one area I have planted *Picea pungens* 'Globosa' (blue globe spruce). A decade ago this puny spruce was barely living, cramped in a five-gallon container. Once planted, it seemed pleased to finally let its roots take off, like snakes spreading into the brown earth. In the early years it was stingy about putting on growth, focusing on movement beneath the ground, securing its roots to the soil. We gardeners need patience. As a rule of thumb, both dwarf and nondwarf conifers spend anywhere from three to six years directing their energies into the root system before substantial growth is seen on top. I see approximately two inches of growth per year on this Buddha-shaped specimen. Its vertical position and sharp, short, strongly blue needles add a textural accent and command attention in the garden.

Adjacent to this spruce is an oval bed of two-foot-tall *Iris orientalis* (butterfly iris). They have purple-and-yellow flowers in early summer. Later in summer and fall, the long yellow leaves look flamboyant next to the spruce. Added to this duo is *Viburnum carlesii* (Korean spice viburnum). As summer vanishes into fall, its leaves turn a rich red. These three plants eloquently express the grandeur that is possible when complementary lines, colors, and textures are ingeniously spun together.

Be aware when you're buying any of the cute dwarf conifers that some are picky and need special placement. Near my patio I have a dwarf spruce—*Picea abies* 'Little Gem'. And what a gem it is! Dense and dome-shaped, it is barely two feet by two feet, with diminutive needles a quarter of an inch long. It is tucked near a two-ton polished-looking granite boulder that, along with assorted perennials and shrubs, gives it needed protection from baking summer and winter sun. It would surely die if it did not have this protection. Because of its evergreen attire, it is pleasing all year round. It catches my attention in the wintertime while I meander through the garden on chilly days, looking for eloquent plant combinations. I occasionally bend over, admire it up close, and stroke its soft needles.

During spring, another nearby plant emerges as a new player on the field. A sunrose (*Helianthemum* red), approximately twelve inches in height, snuggles up to the evergreen, bonding with it. Depending on the kind of winter we are having, this perennial or subshrub (over a span of about five years it gets woody and often needs to be replaced) can be evergreen. Although both plants are green, their shapes and textures are quite different. When blooming, the sunrose, with its assorted circular bright pastels such as pink and double apricot, looks beautiful paired with the evergreen. I like the flare when these two plants are brought together. They would be beautiful on their own, but I added still another plant to this partnership, increasing the dramatic visual appearance of the area. The third plant is *Oenothera acaulis* (evening primrose), a colorful yellow rosette–forming perennial that presses closely to the foliage of the evergreen and the flowers of the sunrose. Even alone, the oenothera is attractive, with its wide, squarish, cup-shaped blooms. But when the duo becomes a trio, there is major transformation. Each element or plant, naturally gardenworthy alone, reaches a higher fusion nestled close to its comrades. A remarkable change for the better has occurred, which is just what my imagination strives toward.

Three other dwarf conifers bring a sense of togetherness to the rock garden on the back perimeter of my property. Designwise they are all strategically placed to add grandeur and ornamentation with the other plants. *Pinus cembra* 'Blue Mound' is a miniature blue form of Swiss stone pine (although, in my opinion, it seems as though someone forgot to brush on the blue paint). The attractive long, soft needles, as well as the bendable branches, are a dark, intense green that contrasts with the firm and muted tones of the granite rock surrounding it. After six years, its shape is conical, four feet tall with a spread of two feet, which is supposed to be its maximum size. I will watch it closely, pruning if necessary to control its size.

In summertime, one of the smaller plants blooming beneath this dwarf evergreen is *Origanum libanoticum* (Lebanese oregano). Streams of one-inch-long, shrimplike pink flowers cascade down and around this four-foot-high rock garden, complementing the robust conifer. Also in the area I have again used silvery *Tanacetum densum* subsp. *amani* (partridge feather). This popular, lacy-foliaged plant, with its yellow-button flowers, complements the oregano as well as the evergreen. All three of these plants pack a visual wallop!

Also providing great pleasure to the eyes are two other evergreens situated within a few feet of each other. Jammed between two rough rocks is *Chamaecyparis pisifera* 'Sungold'. Its juniperlike foliage is midgreen and the tips are dotted with specks of gold. This round loaf-shaped evergreen is four feet wide and two feet tall. After it had been growing for a few years, I was told by a nursery salesperson that it would get fairly large, meaning three or four feet tall. Luckily, so far, it has not overwhelmed its allotted space. Actually, it looks completely appropriate, as a few of the branches dangle over a narrow path with red rocks like guards stationed on either side, appearing to hold it in place.

Below the wispy branches of the conifer is a wide area draped in an unknown species of dianthus. Its alarming red color is luminous in spring; as I hunch over and rub the foliage, I sniff the cinnamon-spicy flowers. Close to the dianthus and the conifer is a more upright form of oregano named *Origanum laevigatum* 'Herrenhausen'. This lightly scented twelve-inch version has purple-green foliage and, in late summer and fall, rosettes of flowers that are deep purple to almost black, maintaining this rich color throughout the fall, until snow floats down and seals its fate.

Snow does not faze *Juniperus squamata* 'Blue Star', which looks marvelous when parts of its foliage are dusted with or partially buried under snow. This shrub offers shades of blue not seen in the other two evergreens. Planted between a flat, rosy boulder and an angular gray stone, this compact juniper has silvery blue needles. It is an influential player in the garden because it adds bulk and it is evergreen, which balances it against the plethora of perennials that swirl around this area. This three-by-three foot shrub has worked fine in this full-sun situation, but it would perform equally well in light shade.

No matter what the season, these dwarf conifers bring a real presence to any garden. They can be counted on to add diversity, as well as a treasure of alluring textures and structural accents, to the home landscape.

Sunny Conclusions

So, although the sun can provide its difficult moments as we sweat in the garden and the temperature rises, its advantages outweigh its drawbacks. I'm grateful to have a full-sun backyard where I can mix and match plants galore, mingling silver plants with various shrubs, eriogonums, and penstemons. Because I'm a major fan of ornamental grasses, I like the linear, silver-blue lines of *Helictotrichon sempervirens* (blue avena or blue oat grass) and the way it blends so well with circular-flowered perennials, such any of the euphorbias, echinaceas, and rudbeckias. Using a host of dwarf bulbs, I also successfully achieve splashes of color and textural combinations as I let my imagination go wild. The intense rays of the sun create a marvelous environment for both sun-loving plants and the gardener's wildest imagination.

The wavy petals and pointed leaves of rose 'Alika' help accent the pastel flowers
of *Stachys grandiflora* 'Superba' (big betony).

CHAPTER THREE

Roses on Parade

Historical Background

*T*he rose has been adored—and sometimes worshipped—through the ages. What other flower has been so constant in our gardens and our hearts? Other plants come and go, traveling up and down the ladder of popularity, but generally, roses remain at the top. What is so alluring about the rose? Some say it's the perfume; others believe it's the colorful blooms or how well roses combine with a variety of other plants. Every person has his or her own particular reason why the rose charms them. For me, it's all of the above, plus the rich variety

Above: The purple clump of *Muscari armeniacum* 'Blue Spike' (grape hyacinth) looks lovely nestled near the rock and hips of *Rosa eglanteria* (sweetbriar).

of blossom forms, the interesting rose hips, and even the diverse shapes and colors of the thorns. But in addition to the plants themselves, I love the rose's historical background.

Through millennia, roses have woven themselves into our psyches and our lives. We find rose stories in mythology, religion, and literature. For example, in ancient times, the rose was the symbol of the god of love, Eros (and, coincidentally, rearranging the letters in his name spells "rose"). From Greek and Roman times to William Shakespeare and Empress Josephine (born Marie Josèphe *Rose* Tascher de La Pagerie), roses have had a place in our lives. According to Ann Reilly, author of *The Rose*, Shakespeare mentions roses more than sixty times in his writings. One of his best known lines comes from *Romeo and Juliet*: "What's in a name? That which we call a rose by any other name would smell as sweet." Perhaps this phrase is in reference to the enduring fragrance old roses are famous for. While Napoleon was busy with military affairs, his wife, Empress Josephine, created a huge collection of Old Garden roses and species roses at their chateau, La Malmaison, in France. Her garden was one of the finest in the country. Napoleon helped contribute to the cause while on his travels by sending seeds and plants back to his wife. Throughout the nineteenth century, France reigned supreme as the home of the best roses.

I learned in *The Quest for the Rose* by Roger Phillips and Martyn Rix that Crusaders brought new roses to Europe from the Middle East in the fourteenth century. Closer to home, a thirty-five-million-year-old rose fossil was found in Florissant, Colorado, just up the road from my garden. A number of years ago, while attending a rose conference sponsored by Heirloom Old Garden Roses nursery in St. Paul, Oregon, I heard people say, "Old roses are affordable antiques." I wholeheartedly agree. For ten or twenty dollars, today's gardener can grow a sentimental piece of the past. Some people buy these roses because they remind them of their childhoods. They like reminiscing about roses that grew in their grandparents' gardens of years ago, along with other old-fashioned flowers such as bells of Ireland, pot marigolds, and Canterbury bells. They are attracted to the charm, character, and fragrance of these old-fashioned roses.

Classification of roses can be quite complex, with disagreement coming even from experts in the field. Generally speaking, Old Garden roses are those types that existed before 1867, which is when the Hybrid Tea rose was introduced to commerce. (Such rose classes as Bourbons, Chinas, and Hybrid Perpetuals are considered Old Garden roses.) Hybrid Teas have been much in the forefront of rose gardening from that time until the last thirty years or so, when the public became more knowledgeable about and desirous of easy-care roses. Now Hybrid Teas are taking a back seat to shrub roses and Old Garden roses. Some roses are easy to grow, while others are more temperamental. Personally, I like the easy ones, which work with my lackadaisical gardening style. I don't grow any Hybrid Teas, which require more attention than I want to give them. They get a host of diseases, need quite a bit of pampering, and, unless well mulched over winter (or even when well mulched), may need to be replaced annually in colder regions of the country.

Approximately half of all Old Garden roses have one exuberant flush of bloom in June, which lasts from a few days to a few weeks; the rest of them have some repeat bloom. Because of this limited span of performance, rose breeders in recent decades have focused on bringing new versions of Old Garden roses to the market. Breeding programs from around the world offer roses with qualities that gardeners want, including hardiness, repeat bloom, and disease resistance. Many of these newer roses combine the strong form and fragrance of the Old Garden roses with the beauty, color, and repeat bloom of the Hybrid Teas. Winter dieback of canes differs from variety to variety and depends heavily on snow cover, soil conditions, rose location, and winter protection. But even in a difficult winter, many shrub roses can be counted on to bounce back (especially if they are grown on their own roots rather than grafted), to perform well, and to require minimal care. I will talk more about these newer roses and how they perform for Western gardeners later on in this chapter.

Species, or wild, roses number in excess of three hundred and are distributed across Europe, Asia, the Middle East, and North America. These roses customarily have five petals, except for *Rosa sericea* and *R. sericea pteracantha*, which have four. Deviation from the five-petal form may have been brought about by accidental mutations and spontaneous crossing of species in the wild. Further naturally occurring pollination among these variations resulted eventually in semi-double (six to twenty petals) and double (more than twenty petals) forms. Humans selected these forms by growing them from seed, and then preserving the types they liked best by asexual reproduction — that is, by rooting cuttings or by grafting.

European or Old Garden roses include the following categories: Gallicas, Damasks, Albas, Centifolias, and Moss roses. Paralleling the evolution of European roses, evidence shows that the Chinese have been growing roses since as early as the tenth century. Over time, some of the Asian species and cultivars found their way into Europe. Crossing these with the Old Garden roses led to the emergence of more old rose classes: Bourbons, Noisettes, Perpetual Damasks, Hybrid Perpetuals, Teas, and Chinas. All these roses have positive and negative attributes, depending on your point of view. Simply put, they are usually strongly fragrant, except for the China roses, which have little scent, and they display various degrees of suckering. (Suckers are canes that spring from below the ground and may need to be removed.) The Hybrid Perpetuals, Bourbons, and Damasks have differing amounts of repeat bloom throughout the growing season, thanks to their Asian genetic inheritance. I stay away from growing Noisettes, Teas, and Chinas, because without protection they are usually too tender for sections of the country where temperatures go below 20° Fahrenheit.

**The delicate, curved blossoms of *Rosa spinosissima*
play-off well next to the fine-textured leaves.**

The colors of the European Old Garden roses range from magenta and purples through shades of pink to ivory white. Some have striped flowers, which are appealing to gardeners wanting something whimsical yet attractive. Their height ranges from roughly three to six feet or more, and they can be especially long lived. Growth habits of the old roses vary widely. Some arch, others climb, some sprawl, others grow mostly upright, and some, such as *R. wichurana*, are even groundcovers, which are excellent for erosion control or used en masse to cover a slope or a difficult site.

After more than a decade of being consumed with rock garden plants, I was ready for something different—and bigger. Browsing through the catalog of classes at the Denver

Botanic Gardens, I spontaneously decided to take a peek at roses and attended some classes. I was curious as to the constant uproar about roses. I experimented with 'Helen Traubel', a Hybrid Tea with tapered buds in shades of sparkling apricot and pink. I tried a few others, whose names I have forgotten, probably because they perished rather quickly.

The classes I took focused heavily on the intense care these roses needed in terms of ridding the plant of thrips, spider mites, botrytis, and many other unpronounceable diseases. Major winter care was also recommended. I remember in one class the instructor was totally covered with protective outerwear to shield her from inhaling dangerous fumes. A bit shocked, I made a quick dash for the door, and a smart decision not to grow these roses anymore!

It was then that I began exploring, through research and library books, if there might be other roses that would work in our roller-coaster climate without a lot of coddling. Soon, I was thrilled to discover Old Garden roses, in addition to a catchall category known as shrub roses, as well as the Canadian roses and hardy Buck varieties. There are hundreds of choices for rose lovers who live in harsh climates. These shrubs not only "work" in the Intermountain region, but also have a lust for life and exhibit profuse blooms.

Each rose, like a person with her own distinctive personality, has traits and shapes to call its own. Most of these roses have varying degrees of winter dieback on the canes; some have none, and others exhibit a lot of brown canes once spring has truly settled in. But the bottom line is that they are tough and resilient, and *nearly all of them* come back to bloom radiantly once the season kicks in. Some flower for a few weeks, while others are more generous with their waterfalls of colors. In my garden, with a hit-or-miss attitude about bloom time, color, and size of the flower, roses are in bloom from late April into November, with the major gift of color pouring out in June. Fragrance, too, is not in short supply. Whether it's mail order or just a garden center around the corner, I purchase what strikes my fancy or gives me inspiration when I read articles and books that propel a particular rose into the spotlight.

Early One-Time Bloomers

In this section I would like to take the reader through my garden as I describe the one-time bloomers and how they perform in my partially shaded front garden. (When I speak of one-time bloomers or once-blooming roses, it means that the rose has one flush of colorful bloom, usually in June. This flush lasts for a few weeks, and then its cycle is completed until the following season.) Blooming for about three weeks in mid-May is one of my first species rose acquisitions, the ancient *Rosa spinosissima*, or *Rosa pimpinellifolia* (Scots rose). It is located close to the south side of my front garden, where it receives abundant sunshine, although it is tolerant of some shade. Generally, shrub roses flourish in full-sun situations, requiring at least six hours of sun; however, the rugosas, the Albas, and some of the species roses, such as the vigorous white-flowered *R. multiflora* and *R. complicata*, with its large, single, rose-pink blooms, tolerate less sun or grow well in dappled shade. Experience is the best teacher. If you notice your rose not blooming profusely or the canes stretching to reach the sun, moving the rose might be the best solution. *R. spinosissima* grows to almost five feet and is smothered with dainty white single blooms. Each slightly cupped bloom is ornamented in the center with showy yellow stamens that offer a pleasant scent. The form is vaselike, with thin stems, tiny prickles, and mid-green foliage that is coarse and fernlike. The Scots rose is appealing in fall, when the foliage turns bronze with tints of yellow and orange; sometimes it is even blessed with unusual small black rose hips. Another little-known variety with plump, purplish black rose hips is *R. spinosissima* 'Altaica' (a.k.a. 'Grandiflora'). Its three-inch flowers are creamy ivory, tinged with butter yellow. Either of these would make a lovely low hedge, especially when planted in front of the reddish purple lilac *Syringa vulgaris* 'Charles Joly', since they bloom at the same time.

Another plus for *R. spinosissima* is its extreme hardiness—not surprising, as its natural habitat extends from Iceland to eastern Siberia into the Caucasus and Armenia. I never have any dieback on the stems, so the only maintenance it needs is to trim out crowded stems every two or three years.

Near this rose is *Cytisus* x *praecox* 'Allgold' (Allgold broom). This large shrub, with its narrow, evergreen stems and yellow pealike flowers, makes a cinematic backdrop to *R. spinosissima*. Beneath the rose is a bed of *Lamium maculatum* 'White Nancy' (dead nettle). Known for its silver-variegated leaves, it is an excellent underplanting and companion for the rose, especially when its white flowers bloom. Sometimes the blooms of the rose are so abundant that the stems bend under the weight and the rose petals rest on the foliage of the groundcover.

Also in this partially shaded front garden is *R.* x *alba* 'Alba Semiplena'. In colder regions of the country, Alba roses grow on average from four to seven feet. In warmer areas they can reach fifteen feet! They are hardy and vigorous, with gray-green leaves and canes heavily armed with thorns. I have placed my 'Alba Semiplena' in a corner, on a slight mound that magnifies its graceful and arching habit. Its deliciously fragrant blooms are produced in clusters of the purest white, which open to show golden-yellow centers. Close to this rose I grow *Geranium psilostemon*, whose long stems wind their way through the rose foliage. The circular flowers are magenta with a dark center. This geranium has large, deeply toothed leaves that turn bronzy red in fall. Another perennial companion to 'Alba Semiplena' is *Sidalcea candida* (checker-mallow). It grows to almost four feet, with a profusion of small, single white flowers that bloom up and down the stems. The plant is somewhat pointed at the tip, so it resembles a short steeple. Plant a few of these together for a lovely visual effect. *Eremurus stenophyllus* (foxtail lily), a magnificent perennial, blends perfectly with the white rose. I like the Eiffel Tower form of this flower. Mine is yellow, but a stunning pastel shade would also combine beautifully.

In late summer into fall, 'Alba Semiplena' produces many inch-long, bottle-shaped red hips that hang on long into the following spring, gradually becoming prunelike and darker red. A nice combination for these rose hips would be *Achillea* 'Moonshine' (yarrow), with its flat yellow flowerheads above silvery dissected foliage.

Species roses also provide magnificent color and vitality in my backyard. First, even before *Rosa spinosissima* blooms in my front garden, the lightly perfumed *R. hemisphaerica rapinii* is totally covered with one-inch single yellow blossoms. After four or five years, the flowers are followed by small, shiny, apple-red rose hips. The yellow flowers last for more than two weeks in early May (and sometimes even begin at the end of April). For a powerful effect, I followed an inner inkling and planted it at the bottom of a berm, where it is very visible as I walk by, adding a sparkling sunny glow early in the season. To accentuate this sunshine-yellow rose, next year I plan to plant a sea of *Veronica oltensis*, whose small green, oak-shaped leaves form a mat topped with sky-blue flowers that bloom simultaneously with the rose.

Next to arrive on the scene is *Rosa xanthina* f. *hugonis* (Father Hugo's Rose). Knowing that this rose will get more than eight feet high and as wide, I gave it sufficient room when I planted it. The canary-yellow single blooms are lovely, although they bloom for less than a week in my garden. However, its bronzy-orange ferny foliage in fall and its fountainlike form compensate for this slight deficit. As my specimen matures it will bear small, dark-red rose hips. *R. foetida* 'Persiana', with its single to semi-double golden yellow flowers, is next in line. "Foetida" translates from Latin into "stinky"! Personally, I find the scent unpleasant; however, other people have told me they do not find it offensive. This rose helps frame my backyard. I have it secured against my back fence, where it reaches about seven feet in height, surrounded by a multitude of shrubs and perennials that enhance its appearance. Toward the front of this border I have silver shrubs such as *Seriphidium canum* (silver sage). A pleasing perennial with *Seriphidium canum*, as well as with the rose, is *Phlomis alpina*, dressed in tiered shades of lavender on tall spires. I was pleased when *Iris lactea* accidentally seeded itself in this bed, as it adds more pale lavender to the picture. In June and July my many grasses are beginning their rise to power; at this stage they are rich shades of green, and add intriguing curvy lines against the globular shapes of the roses.

The other yellow rose that has fascinated me for years is *Rosa* x *harisonii* (Harison's yellow rose—also known as "The yellow rose of Texas"). I like knowing that it was discovered by an attorney living on a farm in Manhattan, New York. (Yes, at one time there were farms in Manhattan!) It is believed to be a cross between two species roses, *R. foetida* and *R. spinosissima*. In the mid-1800s this rose traveled across our wide country with homesteaders, who plopped it into unamended ground wherever they settled. This ruthless treatment is a strong testament to its rugged character; it can withstand neglect and brutal treatment and still shine like a star. In fact, the yellow species roses seem to prefer gravelly soil and little water once established; too much water in too heavy a soil can kill them off.

I first saw this rose a few years back, overflowing with intense double yellow flowers to almost two inches on beautiful large, arching stems, in a busy area with many townhouses. Its billowing habit can span six feet or more in height and width. It was skillfully situated near a corner where it was well viewed not only by visitors in their cars but also by travelers walking on a path near it. They were watchful of its prickly demeanor, so as not to be tackled by a barrage of thorns! If you have a large area to cover or desire a thicket, this would be a good

The intense color of *Geranium psilostemon* (cranesbill) is dramatically enhanced when placed in the center of the explosive *Rosa* x *harisonii.*

For a few weeks in June rose 'Madame Hardy' produces voluptuous trusses of pure white flowers.

choice. Within a few years your dream of tons of blooming roses—even if they last for only about two weeks—will come true.

In my landscape I have used this rose as a backdrop to one of my rock gardens, where I have a plethora of brightly colored plants, including dianthus, penstemons, and eriogonums For a shrubby effect I have included *Ephedra nevadensis* (Mormon tea), with its blue-green needles. Another plant in this rock garden is *Papaver triniifolium* (Armenian poppy). I came across this frilly, peachy-salmon flower one spring when I was a volunteer at the Denver

Botanic Gardens Rock Alpine Garden. I was given some seed, which I immediately, with a carefree approach, sprinkled around my own garden. Within a few years, my garden was beaming with this poppy. A biennial, it begins its growth to stardom as a silvery, fine-textured rosette that is anywhere from five to fifteen inches across. In early spring or summer, as I peer outside, I see dew that has settled on the hairy, glaucous foliage, giving it a glistening appearance. When I flash back to childhood, it reminds me of a dainty doily used to adorn and protect armchairs in our living room.

This poppy has also settled near my patio, where I have another delightful species rose. *Rosa eglanteria* (sweetbriar) was widely used by settlers in early America as a protective hedge and screen. Thomas Jefferson made effective use of this and other species roses at his hilltop mansion, Monticello, near Charlottesville, Virginia. Even before his house was completed and he moved in in 1770, he was diligently planning his garden: In 1767 he planted seedlings of sweetbriar. Jefferson was a prolific gardener, as Monticello attests, and in 1782 he recorded a crimson species rose in flower from May 20 to July 25. A famous quote of Jefferson's (cited in Betts and Perkins's *Thomas Jefferson's Flower Garden at Monticello*) is

> *I have often thought that if heaven had given me a choice of my position and calling, it should have been on a rich spot of earth, well-watered, and near a good market for the production of the garden. No occupation is so delightful to me as the culture of the earth, and no culture comparable to that of the garden...I am still devoted to the garden. But though an old man, I am but a young gardener.*

I agree with this perspective wholeheartedly! Even today, no matter what one's life revolves around professionally, gardening can sweep our hearts away as we devote a portion of our lives to this fun and rewarding endeavor.

Rosa eglanteria is a huge, spiderlike plant. At its maximum, it stretches eight to ten feet with a spread almost as wide. It would be ideal as a privacy hedge, signaling people to stay back. Its strong prickly thorns mangle clothes and scratch skin; the gardener needs arm protection when attending to its maintenance. If you're not using it as a hedge, you can tie its canes loosely to a strong trellis or an arbor. Roses do not cling naturally to hardscape materials, but they can gradually be trained and coaxed to climb and twist up an arbor. If this rose is left on its own, perhaps on the top of a large berm, the huge arching canes can tumble over the garden or mingle with other perennials. A gardener has many choices with *R. eglanteria*, depending on the desired effect. A definite plus for this unusual shrub is the fragrance of its leaves; when gently rubbed between the fingers, they leave a hint of apple scent in the air. The scent is most abundant in the warm moist air of spring, which is also when this shrub produces small, single, clear-pink flowers from top to bottom; the blooms last for a few weeks. The new growth is the most fragrant, so shearing the hedge to promote new growth will increase the amount of fragrance.

The hips of this rose are startling and unique. They start out a glorious pea-sized yellowish green in August—I've never seen any other shrub rose have this look—and gradually, as fall moves in, turn a stunning orange-red; later they become deep red. In fall the rose foliage turns yellow, which is spectacular in contrast with the bright red hips and with the background of my blue-painted house. Even in the depths of winter, the red hips hold fast to the bush. As spring approaches, the hips, now dried like raisins, have not loosened their grip; they remain unfazed to herald the spring season when double grape hyacinths, with their welcome purple color, emerge beneath the shrub.

In my summer garden, my eyes are constantly drawn to the rose 'Hiawatha'. A gift from a friend, it was heartily welcomed into my garden family. To find out more about it, I chatted with the nurseryman who originally sold it to my friend. He had purchased it in the late 1970s from a nursery back East but wasn't sure of its origin before that. I researched it further and learned that it had been bred in 1904 by an American rose breeder named Walsh from Woods Hole, Massachusetts. In my garden this semi-evergreen rose crawls over a rough low granite wall, fanning out to twelve feet (and will probably spread even more as it matures). As it travels across the wall, near a highly visible path, it dips and creeps among the stones, rooting naturally wherever it touches soil. The pliable stems have attractive, glossy green foliage as well as hooked thorns. The flower when it first opens is a single cupped apple-red with ruffled edges, accented at the very center by yellow stamens. As it continues to bloom, the red petals turn a deep rosy shade blotched with white in the middle. It blooms prolifically, in clusters of six or eight, for a few weeks beginning in early summer. Occasionally during its blooming period two plants, one a low sedum with yellow flowers and the other a Colorado wildflower, *Erigeron divergens*, poke through its green leaves. The yellow sedum and the lavender-white pinwheel flowers of the erigeron spontaneously bring more punch to the scene.

'Hiawatha' is a first-class rose that is underused in gardens. As a groundcover it is dense and would be advantageous for erosion control and blocking out weeds. (There are two opinions regarding these groundcover roses; some gardeners say they are useful as weed barriers, while others find them a nuisance to weed around because of the thorns.) This rose would also be a knockout sight scrambling up a tree—for instance, *Crataegus ambigua* (Russian hawthorn), with its white flowers in spring. For me, 'Hiawatha' reflowers briefly in the fall, which is an unusual and pleasant surprise. To add to its many superior qualities, in fall, a few sections are covered with dark red oval hips with a blackish dot at their tips.

Rosa foetida 'Persiana' arches in the background. In the center are
the rich purple-red flowers of rose Hansa. Near the rose are the light purple blooms
of *Iris lactea*, in addition to the silvery foliage of *Seriphidium canum* (silver sage).

Gallicas, grown by the Greeks and Romans, are exceptional choices for Northern gardeners. Known for their tough constitution, these one-time bloomers come in bold colors such as crimson, burgundy, and plum, and have stems that are erect and stiff. Try 'Alika', a semi-double crimson one or the striped variety called rosa mundi (*Rosa gallica* 'Versicolor'), which is splashed white, pink, and crimson. With their low stature (most are under four feet), they are knights in shining armor for gardens of all sizes, even those with some shade. Other superb Gallica selections are 'Cardinal de Richelieu', with its double blooms of smoky purple and velvet texture on almost thornless stems, and 'Charles de Mills', colored crimson-purple to dark lilac, which I have a five-foot specimen of in my front garden. Perennial companions for these hot colors are *Alchemilla mollis* (lady's mantle), various artemisias, santolinas, and the tall *Thalictrum flavum* subsp. *glaucum* (meadow rue), with its powder-puff yellow flowers. To soften the glitzy colors of these roses, use the feathery, pale blue annual *Nigella damascena* (love-in-a-mist). I particularly like *N. damascena* 'Miss Jekyll' because its flowers are a deeper shade of blue than those of the species.

Creatively mixing plant materials, as with the rose and the grape hyacinths, is pleasurable and challenging. Sometimes I plan my plant-palette ideas, but more frequently I work in a most serendipitous manner. When I look at history, I am encouraged that I am not alone in my spontaneous style. Over time, some of the most important scientific ideas did not fit the facts as they could be demonstrated, and the scientists doing their research had to persist with their visions. According to James Newton, author of *Uncommon Friends*, Thomas Edison is a good example. Many people of his time thought of him as a wizard. They often wondered how he came up with his inventions and ideas. While chatting with colleagues he mused about how solutions jumped out at him and said that he relied on his impulses and intuition. Edison did several thousand experiments, which often did not produce the results he was seeking. But he never gave up hope, and knew that the answer was "out there."

Rose 'Hiawatha' spreads her long tentacles along the rockwall as *Euphorbia sequieriana* (spurge), in the upper left hand corner, adds contrast to the scene with its lime-yellow florets.

In this same vein, I think of the English roses first developed by David Austin over thirty years ago. Before he came on the rose scene, rose fanciers either favored the modern roses, which characteristically bloomed an entire season in a wide range of colors, or the Old Garden roses, with their bushy forms, strong perfume, and few weeks of bloom in June. Mr. Austin wove these two sets of distinct characteristics together, and a new rose class emerged. In his book *David Austin's English Roses*, he states that he had not envisioned how popular his roses would be with gardeners worldwide. I am sure many rosarians and horticulturists decades ago didn't believe in Mr. Austin's vision, but luckily he had confidence and persevered. Culturally, even at the end of this second millennium, with so many technological advances, we are shy about admitting the strength and importance of our intuition and creative outbursts. A wealth of knowledge arises from this center within us, where ideas churn, cook, and come to fruition.

Most Austin roses grow five feet and under for Northern gardeners. These include 'Constance Spry'™, which blooms once with double pink flowers, and 'Graham Thomas'™, with double yellow blossoms that repeat through the summer. In addition there is 'Heritage'™, a classically shaped old-fashioned rose that produces full, soft-pink blossoms that repeat well throughout the season; it is known for its strong fragrance. Finally there is the bushy 'Fair Bianca'™, a repeat bloomer, which is similar to the famous once-blooming old variety 'Madame Hardy'. 'Fair Bianca'™ has highly fragrant double blooms colored pale yellow and creamy white. The only Austin I grow is 'Queen Nefertiti'™, which I purchased because of its Egyptian name. It is a soft, tight-centered double yellow brushed with apricot. Under two feet, it reliably repeats and makes a compact, tidy bush. Planted near a flower-patterned wrought-iron bench, it adds a pleasant feel to my garden. In the Intermountain region and Midwestern states, many Austin roses need winter protection; check with other gardeners and experts in your area to see how certain varieties have performed. Although many Northern gardeners grow these Austin roses, I believe more testing is needed to thoroughly determine their hardiness over time.

Using intuition in my garden, I pair contrasting materials, such as foliage, texture, seedheads, stems, and flowers, as well as stone, rocks, and paths. I create appealing compositions that lure the garden visitor first to peek in and then to stroll further within my garden walls and paths. Contrast, used with restraint and diversity, is an ongoing theme in my garden. For example, I like to mix perennials, annuals, and shrubs to provide an abundance of leafy plant material. Many of these plants are large, with smaller varieties placed toward the front. I diversify the scene with masses of colored stones, boulders, and paths. The stones are used in my artistically designed rock gardens and strategically situated rock walls, where smaller, more delicate plants complement the larger-scale plant material in my various borders. Shrub roses and other dazzling perennials, when united to beautify the landscape, behave like dancing partners. They appear to take turns as to who is in the lead. From moment to moment my eyes shift their focus, gazing with delight from one plant or grouping to another.

In addition to providing color, height, and diverse shapes, perennials and annuals that are grown with roses have another use. Over time, many old roses and the larger shrub roses develop strong trunks or "knobby knees." When flowers are added at the base, they cover up these bare spots.

More Hardy Roses

After the explosive fireworks displays of the one-time bloomers, a wide variety of other roses decorate my garden in summer and fall. I am fond of the rugosa roses, which bloom in early summer with various amounts of repeat bloom, sometimes concurrent with the one-time bloomers. *Rosa* 'Hansa' has been a mainstay with me for a number of years. As *R. foetida* 'Persiana' is winding down, 'Hansa', which grows to about four feet, is taking off with its full, vibrant purple-crimson colors. In autumn it also has a nice crop of scarlet rose hips. Now and then it flowers at the same time as the fragrant hybrid musk rose 'Nymphenburg', which has fluffy semi-double salmon-pink flowers with lemon and deeper pink tones. Its thick, slightly arching canes reach six feet in my garden. To complement these roses I use silver plants and ornamental grasses such as *Calamagrostis* x *acutiflora* 'Karl Foerster' (feather reed grass). The deep-green vertical leaves, with their emerging plumose tops, create a kaleidoscopic vision.

The next two roses have *Rosa rugosa* as one of their parents, but strictly speaking they are classified as shrub roses. The first is 'Corylus', a rose from England that I bought many years ago. It grows to three feet near my patio, with silvery pink single flowers and stems covered with profuse small prickles. While I like its pleasant fragrance and the fact that it reblooms for me in the fall, what I find most appealing is its foliage. Most rugosas have foliage that is thick and highly textured, but the leaves of 'Corylus' are elongated and more delicate. In fact, its rugosa parentage is not apparent without close examination. The leaves shine in fall with muted tones of gold, orange, and burgundy. Flanking this rose I grow *Deschampsia caespitosa* (tufted hair grass), which adds bright green color and diversifies the picture with its dense mound of narrow foliage.

The second rose with some rugosa characteristics is 'Basye's Purple Rose'. I'm a sucker for blue- and purple-flowered plants of any kind. I had seen pictures of this rose, with its velvety reddish purple blossom, so when I saw it at a rose sale, I knew I had to buy it.

Even though Dr. Robert E. Basye bred this rose in the warmer climate of Texas in 1980, he was known to raise rugosa hybrids that were hardy, as well as being drought tolerant. At this stage in its young life my plant is only about two feet tall, with dark reddish purple stems but no blooms as yet. I'm hopeful that the single blooms will appear this year and I can enjoy their uncommon color and fruity fragrance.

In regard to fragrance, in my opinion, nothing tops *Rosa rugosa* 'Alba'. I've been growing this rose for a long time. It is planted right next to a woodland path, receiving plenty of sun (which it thrives on, although it would do well in a lightly shaded situation too). Every time I walk near, I take in its powerful scent, which is evocative of a sweet floral perfume. The single white blooms are splashed with yellow centers. Unlike most rugosa roses, mine has not spread aggressively. Perhaps that is because I did not amend the soil much, and it grows happily in clay, which inhibits its travels. For gardeners who find rugosas too aggressive, I recommend holding back on the addition of organic matter to control their spreading habit.

Rudbeckia fulgida var. *sullivantii* 'Goldsturm' takes center stage as it is engulfed by the feathery plumes of *Deschampsia caespitosa* (tufted hair grass) on the left, and the powerful red glow of rose 'Morden Ruby'. On the far right, the leaves of *Calamagrostis brachytricha* (Korean feather reed grass) bend gracefully.

Thalictrum flavum 'Glaucum' (yellow meadow rue), with its puffy blossoms, almost hides narrow blue flowers of *Salvia nemorosa* (sage). On the far left are the strawberry-red flowers of rose 'Murden Ruby'. Shooting up in the center are the thin lines of *Helictotrichon sempervirens* (blue avena grass), while hugging the lower far left corner is the plummage of *Alchemilla mollis* (lady's mantle).

To pick up on the yellow in the center of the flowers, and to add something different to the planting scene, I grow the groundcover grass *Alopecurus pratensis* 'Aureovariegatus' (yellow foxtail grass) planted casually around this rose. For me it grows under a foot high; its narrow leaves are bright green with vivid yellow longitudinal stripes. The overall effect is strongly golden. Like *Rosa rugosa* 'Alba', this grass is tolerant of a wide range of soils, so it adapts perfectly in this spot.

Over the years, I have noticed only two drawbacks with rugosas. One is their susceptibility to some winter damage. Depending on location, some canes are damaged by heavy snows. This problem is simply solved by pruning these canes to the ground, which stimulates more to emerge. The other problem is the occasional yellowing of foliage due to the lack of iron accessible to the plant in clay soils. But I know this happens with rugosas in sandy soil too. A twice-a-year application of liquid iron in spring and early summer will usually relieve this difficulty. Another option is to fertilize these roses, along with all your others, about once every six weeks, from when they leaf out to mid-August, with a high-quality fertilizer containing iron. But if you don't get around to this chore, a few slightly yellow leaves don't usually detract from the rose's magnificent bloom and scent. Rugosas are also intolerant of any kind of garden spray other than water, so be careful if you must spray herbicides or insecticides near them.

Fertilizing is a complex and highly debated topic among rosarians. Some questions that get bounced around are: Do you want to use chemicals, or an organic mixture, or well-aged manure? How much to put down? When to do it? Liquid or granular? Gardeners add nutrients in an effort to grow bigger and more floriferous roses. Because I have over eighty shrub roses and because fertilizing is a big hassle for me, I rarely do it; over the past thirteen years, I've fertilized only two or three times with Mile-Hi Rose Feed, an organically based rose food that is appropriate for the Rocky Mountain region as well as other regions around the country. Honestly, I haven't noticed whether it has helped or not! Check at your local garden center for options; whatever your choice, I suggest keeping it simple. The Canadian roses I grow—more about these below—have never been fertilized, aside from adding compost in early spring, and their blooms look full and beautiful each year.

Another group highly suited to the colder regions of the West are the Griffith Buck roses. These roses come from Iowa but, though they've been around for about twenty-five years, they've only recently become readily available. Mail-order catalogs are likely your best source, except for the popular 'Carefree Beauty', a four-foot rose with loosely double rose-pink flowers that has some repeat bloom. The Buck rose I have is 'Applejack', which has double pink flowers with light yellow centers. It grows to five feet and, as its name implies, has a light apple scent. There is one strong flush of bloom in spring with some repeat in fall.

I personally like roses that rest a tad in summer so that when they rebloom in fall I am delight-fully surprised!

Panicum virgatum (switch grass), with its breezy and delicate textured plumes, is an agreeable companion to roses, as is practically any other ornamental grass. I also recommend practically any variety of coreopsis to complement the bright and pastel shades of most roses. Their various daisylike faces in shades of gold add cheer throughout the season provided one is faithful about deadheading. Most kinds of coreopsis need this attention, except for two varieties: *Coreopsis verticillata* 'Moonbeam' and *C. verticillata* 'Zagreb'. 'Moonbeam' has been temperamental for me, failing to return reliably even after a mild winter. Mulching may be necessary; since I rarely mulch anything, I don't grow 'Moonbeam' anymore. 'Zagreb' is a better choice for our region. An additional plus is that it is more drought tolerant.

Even more than the hardy Buck roses, I favor the rugged Canadians, particularly the Parkland and Explorer series. These roses come from two breeding programs in Canada and are vigorous and winter hardy when grown on their own roots. (Own-root roses are propagated vegetatively by stem cuttings rather than grafted onto the rootstock of another rose. Plants grown on their own roots are usually longer lived than grafted ones.) I use coreopsis, rudbeckias (coneflowers), and other colorful perennials and ornamental grasses with these. The Canadian roses are a hot item at garden centers because nurserymen have extensively promoted them of late in garden classes. Their virtues include ease of care, and each has additional distinctive traits that gardeners lust after, including disease resistance, winter hardiness, and repeat bloom. Hardy Canadian roses and others that have been tested here over time are ideal candidates for the erratic weather that gardeners in the North experience. Just recently a late spring storm—May 20, to be exact—dumped four inches of snow in the Denver Metro area and temperatures plummeted to thirty degrees F. Many of my perennials were flattened, yet most of my shrub roses came through practically unscathed.

With over forty Canadian varieties to choose from, I'll mention a few that have caught my eye. It took me a few years to become accustomed to the foot-dragging pace of 'Morden Ruby'. In its early years it seemed to just sit there when, as a typical impatient gardener, I was begging it to perform immediately. I always tell enthusiastic gardeners to be patient, and here I was having hysterics after just a few years! Factually, I know it was busy sinking its roots in the ground. 'Morden Ruby' has finally grown to four feet in my garden. In addition to its deep burgundy stems, the dark pink double flowers are distinguished by tiny, almost silvery flecks on the petals. This rose and the highly fragrant Bourbon rose 'Louise Odier', with its camellia-style lilac-pink blossoms, are in the same bed. To add juice to the scenario, I crammed this bed tight with perennials and grasses, but no flowers were as clamorous as these two major hitters, so a delightful juxtaposition sprang up between their colorful loudness and some quieter perennials and grasses. Here I used the softer yellow of *Thalictrum flavum* subsp. *glaucum* (meadow rue) and the dainty grass *Deschampsia caespitosa* (tufted hair grass). Another grass, *Miscanthus sinensis* 'Gracillimus' (maiden grass), soars above. Additionally, from my front garden, I transplanted a piece of *Knautia macedonica,* whose button-sized red flowers go well with the voluptuous blooms of 'Morden Ruby'. Three more perennials—*Achillea* 'Moonshine' (yarrow), *Salvia nemorosa* (ornamental sage), and *Alchemilla mollis* (lady's mantle)—top off this flowery extravaganza.

Another Canadian rose I like to grow because of its petite stature (under two feet) is 'Henry Hudson'. The fragrant, semi-double white flowers with deep yellow centers have a pink tinge and resemble fluffy powder puffs. Use this repeat-blooming rose as a base beneath tall grasses and nearby fall-blooming asters, as well as next to the annual Verbena 'Imagination', known for its carpeting habit and purple flowers. Or try any low annual red or white dianthus. Two more Canadians that I recommend are 'J. P. Connell', the one yellow repeat-flowering variety, and the climber 'John Cabot', which I only recently planted, although it's been around since 1978. I have had a few flowers on it and like its deep red/pink semi-double blooms, which appear on strong, arching canes. It will flower profusely in June and July and then repeat sporadically in August and September. I've found that 'J. P. Connell' needs extensive pruning here in spring because of winter injury. Nevertheless, it recovers well to produce a full flush of flowers in June. Gardeners who love hybrid teas will note that this rose, when it first opens, has the high centered form of the hybrid teas, but later opens wider to expose the stamens and then fades to a cream color.

A totally different Canadian rose is 'Martin Frobisher'. The semi-double blossoms are blush pink with hints of lavender. The almost thornless canes are sturdy, maroon colored, and reach about five feet in height.

Nearby this rose, I planted *Geranium magnificum* (cranesbill), a two-foot mound-forming flower with singular purple flowers etched with darker colored veins. *Papaver triniifolium* springs up in the background, completing the scene with a touch of peach.

A final Canadian rose is 'Adelaide Hoodless'. This rose was named in tribute to the founder of the first Women's Institute in Canada, begun in 1897, on the occasion of its seventy-fifth anniversary. The Institute's purpose, according to Yvonne Cuthbertson, author of *Women Gardeners*, was to broaden the outlook of farm women, educate them, and get them involved in their communities to improve their quality of life. This bushy rose is of high quality and stamina, which I can attest to from experience. In return for a good deed my neighbors did for me, I gave them this rose as a thank-you. They planted it next to their driveway, among cobblestones. Even though it receives no care and no additional water, other than the fifteen or so inches of rain our area receives naturally, it still blooms prolifically every

The large foliage of *Borage officinalis* (borage), on the left, differs from the peasize yellow flowers of Cotula sp., an import from South Africa. *Seriphidium canum* (silver sage), on the right, is balanced by the rich red color of the protruding rose. Rounding out the picture is a natural-looking clay container.

spring and sporadically in fall! At first, local catalogs said it reached four feet, but that needed to be changed when customers noticed that, after a few years, cascading canes grew to six feet with clustered, deep red, semi-double blooms.

Two other groups of roses for Northern gardeners are the Kordeses and the Austins (previously discussed). Wilhelm Kordes, from northern Germany, began developing hardy roses in the 1930s and '40s. They make great short climbers or specimens. His 'Karlsruhe', little known in this country, reaches four feet or more and bears fully double, rosy pink flowers that repeat regularly; as a bonus, the foliage is abundant and glossy green. 'Dortmund' is a single red short climber with a white eye and exceptionally beautiful shiny, hollylike green leaves. 'Sparrieshoop' is a single to semi-double, with trusses of extra-large apple-blossom flowers that are highly perfumed. Kordes roses were used in the breeding of the Canadian roses, which speaks to their hardiness for gardeners in harsh climates. One of the best climbers is at the same time both a Canadian rose of the Explorer series and a Kordes rose. 'William Baffin' has clustered raspberry semi-double blooms, is wide-growing and vigorous, and repeat-blooms. I'm excited to see this rose scurrying up my trellis; in a few years it will overtake my patio, giving me shade and privacy. 'William Booth', another Canadian Explorer rose with Kordes blood, is a single medium-red rose that is fairly new in the nursery trade. It has a spreading habit, repeatedly blooms in clusters, and stays at about three feet high.

As crossbreeding becomes increasingly complex, various roses do not fit exactly into any specific category, but get lumped together under the broad heading of "shrub roses." I grow a few of these and have found that they are quite hardy, with various degrees of cane dieback, depending on the severity of the winter. 'New Face' is another rose whose name beckoned me. Its unusual feature is that the mostly single blossoms are multicolored creamy-yellow, edged in pink, but some are either all white or all pink. Because of its many sprays of blooms on each stem, it is an excellent choice to bring inside for bouquets.

This rose blends easily with other flowers. I adore letting Shirley poppies (*Papaver rhoeas*) seed themselves all over this area. The large, papery thin, red, white, and pink flowers, at three feet, dance below the six-foot, sky-high form of 'New Face'. Even taller than the rose is *Thalictrum flavum* subsp. *glaucum* (meadow rue), which circles among these other two plants. It was originally planted in my front shade garden, but I imagined that its yellow coloring would look stunning with the rose and the poppies, so I moved a small part of it to my backyard garden. This threesome of plants seduces me in high summer. Another plant that adds to this arrangement is *Phlomis russeliana* (Jerusalem sage). I first saw this perennial in Zurich, Switzerland, a decade ago at the Städtische Sukkulenten-sammlung, a botanic garden devoted mainly to succulents. As I mentioned in the introduction to this book, my husband and I studied in Zurich in the 1970s, and in five years of living there I became fond of the people and the surroundings, so when the opportunity to revisit arose, I jumped at the chance to take a nostalgic trip back to my Jungian roots. Of course, since plants were my passion now, I checked out the local botanic gardens, and there this plant was, surrounded by a bed of sempervivums (hens and chicks). It looked queenly and stout with its dense whorls of large, yellow-hooded flowers soaring above the tiny succulents. I was enthralled by its big, robust, rather heart-shaped woolly leaves and knew, upon my return to the States, that I had to purchase this plant.

A rose that was easy to find locally is the climbing miniature 'Jeanne Lajoie'. The double blooms are classically shaped, like those of a hybrid tea, but are only two inches wide, which creates mounds of pink cotton-candy flowers that bloom throughout the season. I'm training this climber to spiral up a sturdy metal trellis with many grasses and yellow daisy flowers circling beneath it.

Growth Habit and Pruning

According to a booklet titled *Roses for the North*, put out by the Minnesota Agricultural Experiment Station, there are eight categories of growth habit for shrub roses and Old Garden roses: arching, climbing, dense, groundcover, suckering, open, rugosa, and spreading. These categories overlap somewhat, depending on how a rose grows in the garden and the care it receives. Some roses fit into two or more categories. For example, *Rosa eglanteria* can be a climber, a spreader, or an archer, depending on the tending it receives. If left without support, it will cascade widely, with tips that bend down to the ground. However, if it is guided up an arch or other structure and carefully pruned, it can be put into the category of climber. As a gardener, you have a fair amount of control over the look you want to achieve.

'Banshee', a fragrant double pink shrub rose of unknown origin, is another good example. In my garden, I let this once-blooming seven-foot-tall rose grow naturally, near the south side of my house. Occasional stem removal keeps it open; it is mostly upright, although halfway up the stems sway outwards. However, in another garden I saw, the gardener had trained it to drape loosely over a white gate, so it can also be called a small climber.

Dense and suckering roses can often be clumped into the same category. Many Gallicas and rugosas are similar. Both are fairly low growing, not reaching over five feet for Northern gardeners. If left unattended, both will display various amounts of suckering, which makes them become dense. Suckering can become a problem depending on your perspective and the site. Do you want more canes to fill in an area or make a hedge, or is the rose, where it is planted, annoying and troublesome?

To avoid confusion, I place groundcovers, ramblers, and climbing roses all in the same category. Remember, we want to keep rose pruning simple. Any rose that produces long, pliable canes can be trained up and around any solid structure. How tall it grows depends on its individual characteristics as well as regional climatic conditions, microclimates, and winterkill. The first season, to buffer it against powerful winter conditions, I suggest three or four shovelfuls of soil over the crown after the ground has almost frozen. (This is around Thanksgiving in my region.) With all newly planted shrub roses I would recommend this

The fluffy pastel pink of rose 'Martin Frobisher' and the airy blooms of *Papaver triniifolium* (Armenian poppy), on the far right, are offset by the smashing color of *Geranium magnificum* (cranesbill).

extra soil treatment for winter protection, especially if you received the rose by mail in a small pot and its roots were small and delicate.

To control the height, growth, and shape of any rose, good pruning techniques are necessary. Generally speaking, most people who are new to gardening or who are working with shrub roses for the first time are baffled and intimidated by the idea of pruning these plants. Pruning is seen as complicated and difficult. While I too felt this way at first, over time I conquered my fear! Honestly, what is the worst that can happen? A wrong stem is cut here or there or the rose is cut too low. Unless it has been butchered extensively (and sometimes even then), it will grow back. It may not look perfect in the current season, but there are always many more years to come. As with many operations, hands-on experience is the best teacher, and improvement comes with practice.

There are many different methods and styles of pruning; each rose book gives slightly different advice, and every gardener has her own crafty ways. With an adventuresome spirit, a nonchalant approach, and sharp tools, I have had much success with my roses. The following few tips will be helpful to the novice rose gardener, but it's important to remember to trust your intuition and to imagine how you want the rose to look artistically among the other plants and features in your garden.

First, if possible, I learn something about the natural growth habit of the rose I'm attempting to shape, so that I can prune it accordingly and it can retain its unique personality. Down the road, this small quantity of research is a good investment. It has helped me avoid such planting mistakes as putting a large, vigorous grower, such as the climbing rose 'American Pillar', with its single, reddish pink flowers, at an entrance to a modest patio, where 'The Fairy', a two-feet-by-two-feet pink rose, would provide a more appropriate fit.

Next, for approximately the first three to five years, I leave my roses alone. During those early years, while the plant's energy is focused underground, I limit pruning to cutting out dead and straggly stems, which take energy from the more vigorous and productive canes. As the rose matures, I delve further into pruning techniques. In late winter or early spring, I begin to look for canes that have died or are diseased or damaged. I also look to thin out some of the oldest canes. To identify these aged stems, look for the thickest ones; they will be mottled, brown, and the surface will be barklike. These older canes often do not bloom well, and eliminating a *few* each year stimulates new growth. With a keen eye, they are easy to spot, since they're a strong contrast to the often thinner, healthy new green stems.

Early May in my region is when I do most of my final pruning on the new growth. At that time I can clearly see the strong delineation between winterkill and new growth. When I cut into the stems, I cut out *all* the bad growth, *plus* I prune a few inches into the new green growth, which again increases the vigor of the rose. This is my basic approach with all my roses.

I have honed a few additional skills over the years. I watch for canes that are crossing each other, which may rub and injure the plant, allowing pests and diseases to filter into the rose. I keep an eye out for canes that are too crowded. Crowding interferes with sunlight and good air circulation, which are critical requirements for healthy growth and blooms. I try to pay attention to buds pointing outward and make each pruning cut a quarter of an inch above such a bud, which encourages the direction of growth outward and contributes to more air and sun reaching the center of the plant. But I don't fuss too much over this point; basically, I trust my inner, intuitive, commonsense approach.

When I attend to once-flowering roses, I attempt to remember to prune them shortly after they have produced their flush of color in June. This allows time for new growth to ripen over summer, resulting in a greater crop of flowers the next year. If I expect (and want) rose hips, I leave the spent flowers alone for the time being. Further pruning can be completed after the hips have fallen or are really ratty looking. However, since I am less busy with gardening in the late winter months, and also because I have many one-time bloomers, I often cut out weak or old canes during these months. I won't get as many flowers next summer, but

I don't mind sacrificing some flowers, since I have plenty of others to enjoy and it's easier to see what needs modifying on the framework of the bush after the leaves have fallen. Each gardener should do whatever works best with his or her roses and lifestyle.

If the rose goes on producing flowers through summer and autumn, pruning is best left until late winter so that one can enjoy as many blossoms as possible. At that time, I will shorten side shoots—sprouts that come off the horizontal parts of the main vertical canes by about one-third, which encourages the production of more flowers. If rose hips are expected from repeat-blooming varieties, then spent flowers are not removed. Some gardeners, like me, enjoy the appearance of the hips, which add diversity and more color to the makeup of the garden late in the season. Other people have fun making rose-hip tea. The taste of rose hips is tart and cranberry-like. They are famous for their high vitamin C content. In addition to teas, rose hips are used in wines, soups, muffins, and jams.

Throughout the growing season, regular deadheading of spent blooms encourages more blossoms on both continuous and repeat bloomers. ("Repeat" means blooming in spring and fall. "Continuous" means cycling approximately every six to eight weeks during the growing season.) When a cluster of flowers has finished blooming, clip off these faded blooms at the appropriate leaf bud, which is usually where there are five leaflets. Do not make this pruning cut where there are three leaflets. The harder pruning, at five leaflets, stimulates active growth, and within a few weeks you will be rewarded with more blooms. (But again, if you want rose hips in the fall, do not practice this technique, especially from midsummer on, so that colorful rose hips can form.) In addition, some roses have spent petals that are messy and woefully sad-looking. Removing them will help your rose maintain a fresh look.

Climbing roses vary a great deal depending on the region you live in. Nowadays, especially with the Canadian roses, breeders are hybridizing varieties that are extremely tolerant of weather variables, so the rose will build up enough height to climb even in cold regions. But often it is still helpful to know something about the rose before you buy it. For instance, despite the fact that 'Dortmund' is a hardy Kordes variety, it generally will not reach twelve feet in the North unless it is grown in a very sheltered area, and even then it is unlikely to grow that tall. On average it will grow to about eight feet.

Any long-caned rose initially needs room to establish itself. After the rose has become established, which is generally in about three to five years, you can gradually begin to train canes on supports if you are not letting them trail over the ground. Use strong, stable structures; flimsy wooden arches are usually insufficient. When the stems are young and pliable, they are easy to maneuver. Gently bend the canes downward and wrap and tie them to where you want them to grow. Use only material with some give to it, such as old nylons or the one-inch-wide green stretch material readily available at garden centers. Never use wire, which would constrict and kill the cane and probably the rose. As the shrub matures, developing more side shoots off the main canes, these can also be cut back, increasing the flower production. Intense pruning of climbers is not necessary; every few years, remove old unproductive growth and weak stems. If you wait much past six or ten years to tackle your climbing rose, canes become less flexible, thicker, and harder to shape. Added to this challenge is the rough treatment thorns give to exposed skin. I'm aware it's smart to bundle my body and hands when I prune a thorny rose; however, I'm often performing another garden chore, and suddenly think to tackle the rose—of course when I'm dressed in shorts. Occasionally my impulsive nature gets me into a bit of a mess. Every so often when I'm pruning roses and yell "Ouch!" I recall what Graham Stuart Thomas said about the unfriendliness of rose thorns in *The Graham Stuart Thomas Rose Book*. His philosophy is that the thorns help accentuate the beauty of roses—offering a parallel to life, with its balance of good and evil.

Above all, however you prune your roses, keep in mind that pruning is an art. It's a creative challenge and an adventure, like painting, drawing, or writing. And, as in those artistic meanderings, follow your inner inklings and common sense. I take my time and never rush, inspecting the rose from a few different angles. I cut, then stand back and, like an artist, look at what I've done and decide whether more is needed this year. Of course, learning a few techniques is helpful, but then let them go. Experiment; have fun in your garden. Gradually you will become more skilled with practice and your confidence will increase. Be patient. Trust yourself. This is not brain surgery on a human! Exactitudes may fit into a few areas of life, but certainly not in the garden. And finally, remember to love gardening, and enjoy the euphoric feeling as you see the results of your artistic undertakings when the roses, like the chorus in a Broadway musical, explode into bloom.

So, whether shrub roses are familiar plants that you have grown for years, or whether you are a beginning gardener, continue to enjoy these wonderful plants—as others have before you and as our children will for centuries to come.

The cottony white flowers of *Filipendula vulgaris* (dropwort) weave in nicely among the sky-blue blossoms of *Consolida ambigua* (annual larkspur) and the red cupped flowers of *Papaver somniferum* (opium poppy). *Digitalis lanata* (foxglove), with its white tonguelike blooms, stand out well in front of the whole panorama.

CHAPTER FOUR

Shimmering in the Shadows: Plants for Shady Sites

ॐ

*R*umors abound on the difficulty of shady sites, and when I had my gardening business I often heard complaints from my clients about shade. Gardeners would do well to let fade into oblivion the myth that one can only grow hostas and *Vinca minor* (periwinkle) in shaded areas. Admittedly, gardeners must research plant selection more studiously for shady sites, but a winning garden can definitely

Above: The mottled foliage of *Pulmonaria saccharata* 'Janet Fisk' (lungwort) contrasts with the tiny blue flowers of *Brunnera macrophylla* (heartleaf brunnera) above the lungwort, as well as *Geranium pyrenaicum* (cranesbill) with its airy purplish flowers on the right.

be achieved without full sun. Indeed, the shade garden can offer as much pleasure as its counterpart, the sunny site. Shade gives us relief from soaring temperatures and from the blistering sun that beats down on our bodies and our precious plants. Shady nooks and patios entice us outdoors, while passionate gardeners can always seek relief beneath a canopy of trees to clean up a portion of the garden where the sun don't shine!

I love my partially shaded garden, which faces east toward the street in my busy suburban neighborhood. My shade garden exists in large part because of my cottonwood tree, a multistemmed giant that casts a shadow on the entire front yard. Aside from *Acer negundo* (box elder), *Populus deltoides* (cottonwood), and the moisture-loving *Salix amygdaloides* (peachleaf willow), which spreads extensively across the middle of the continent, not many trees are native to the Rocky Mountain region. Twenty-five years ago, with a new house and a barren landscape, putting in a cottonwood tree seemed appropriate to me. I wanted a tree that would add structure and knock the temperature down a few notches during the hot summer months. Though some people might see this large tree, and the shade it casts, as a nuisance, I am satisfied with my cottonwood and the ample shade it provides from noon onwards. Each of its five massive stems, twelve inches in diameter, seems especially firmly anchored to the earth. All of its parts are distinctive, from its large waxy leaves to the curves of its corky branches and stems. Its parachute of foliage shelters the hundreds of perennials and shrubs that surround it, adding flavor and spice. These contrasting elements transform the original simple "tree" idea; together, they create an integrated scene, a lushly beautiful shade garden.

After planting the cottonwood, I put in a split-rail fence for aesthetic appeal and structural accent. In the early years of this shade garden, the split-rail fence and the cottonwood were the main elements that I worked around. In addition to providing structure, the fence told the many grade-school and high-school students passing by that my garden was off limits. The fence gave the message "Stay on the path, please!" Mostly, people have. As I weeded and planted during school days, some children even told me that they liked the flowers. Once, while I was taking photographs for the garden classes I teach, on a whim I asked two boys passing by if they would like to be in a shot. Proudly they smiled, looked at each other, and nodded "Yes!" They then stood in front of my fence, with wide grins across their faces. (I bet that at dinnertime they shared the news of their photographic adventure with their family. If I had been really sharp, I would have told them to come back another day and I would have gladly given them a copy of the picture.)

I made some mistakes in the early years of my shade garden. New to the field of gardening, I chose to install two aspens near my front door. Like any new homeowner, I was drawn by their fluttering leaves, so abundant in the mountains, and by the fact that they were for sale at every garden center in Denver! Mistake. Over the years I learned that the best place for these trees is in the mountain communities where they thrive. The elevation agrees with them and in the wild they are less prone to diseases, such as a pest that gets inside the trunk and produces unsightly bulges. Also, at lower elevations, aspen leaves often turn black because of leaf blight. Within a few years, I saw the error of my ways, chopped down the aspens, and surrounded my cottonwood with a wide spectrum of perennials and bulbs. A local gardening personality on the radio jokingly says that the best thing for an aspen is a chain saw!

Casting Shade: A Few Good Selections

Several other trees would offer benefits similar to my cottonwood; however, at this stage in my life I am not patient enough to wait ten or more years for another specimen to mature. If you're younger and more patient than I am, I'd like to suggest a few alternatives. There are many choices of small to medium-size trees. In fact, in the category under twenty feet, there are two that sound so appealing I may change my mind and purchase them! In fact, I did buy a specimen of *Rhamnus frangula* 'Asplenifolia' (fernleaf buckthorn) a few years back, but regrettably lost it. This is an excellent tree for a small shady garden, or for use in a large perennial bed as a dreamy accent plant. Fernleaf buckthorn grows to a maximum height of fifteen feet and spreads only ten feet. It boasts extremely fine-textured, narrow leaves and is unrivaled for the diversity it brings to any landscape. It produces red berries in summer, which turn black in fall to accompany the yellow-orange fall foliage. I can truly imagine this specimen in my back garden, taking center stage in summer and fall. Because of its wispy leaf form, practically any perennial with lush foliage would perk up the scene. I favor the pulmonarias (lungworts), with their long-pointed leaves, white-spotted foliage, and flowers that generally open pink and then turn blue. A choice cultivar is *Pulmonaria* 'Sissinghurst White', with generous white flowers and silver-white spotted leaves. Massed together, these plants add elegance to a shady area. Another excellent selection for awesome texture and color is *P.* 'Excalibur', with rosy flowers and strong silvery white foliage. One that I've grown for a few years is *P. longifolia* 'Bertram Anderson', with violet-blue flowers and dark green leaves spotted with silvery green. I'm particularly fond of pulmonarias because when their small, trumpetlike blooms have finished, the foliage continues to be pleasing and would look glorious beneath any tree. These flowers are easy to grow, as long as they are given adequate moisture. (When the leaves curl and droop, the plant is sending out a signal that it is thirsty; once watered, the leaves become perky again.)

The massed vertical spires of *Digitalis lanata* (foxglove) create elegance, while dappled shade rests on the curved concrete birdbath.

The other small tree that I like is *Ptelea trifoliata* (wafer ash or hop tree). This multi-stemmed tree has a rounded top and clustered white flowers that are deliciously scented, reminiscent of honeysuckle; the leaves too are aromatic. For summer interest the white flowers transform to winged seeds or wafers, and in fall the foliage turns yellow.

One last tree, which may reach twenty-five feet in the West, is *Cornus mas* (Cornelian cherry). I've wanted this one for years and will buy it next time I make a jaunt to a local nursery that's known for unusual and fascinating trees. This small tree or large shrub explodes in late winter/early spring with ethereal clouds of yellow flowers on leafless branches, which gives it a unique appearance. In some years, after the flowers have finished, it has red, cherrylike fruits. Building gardens beneath trees of any size helps dispel

Knautia macedonica dances among the vertical spires of *Echium vulgare* (viper's bugloss)
and the deep purple petals of *Clematis* x *jackmanii.*

the false belief that plants needing various amounts of shade cannot be successfully grown in the West because we just "do" sunny and dry.

Very Vertical

In a shade garden beneath a tree, the first question is, "What plant will both imitate the habit and complement the look of the tree?" Digitalis (foxglove) is one of my first choices. Dramatic straight lines are indispensable for splendor; they also serve as an exclamation point and add spice to the scene. But imitation is only half of the plan; I also use low-growing plants such as hardy geraniums (cranesbills, not annual geraniums), doronicums (leopard's bane), and pulmonarias (lungwort). (The strange common name "lungwort" was used by medieval herbalists, who believed that because the plant resembled a diseased lung, it must be a cure for ailments of that organ.) These cushionlike forms contrast with the vertical display of the foxgloves and also bring in softness and more color, which plays off the densely textured tree trunk. Partial shade is ideal for most forms of digitalis, which are easy to grow in any fertile soil. The common foxglove, *Digitalis purpurea*, is a biennial, meaning that it has a two-year cycle, flowering and producing seed in the second year. However, here in the North it doesn't always come back the second year. I admire the architectural forms of these plants, so I buy various species and place them randomly around my shady sites. They look especially attractive planted in clusters, where they not only add vertical interest but are positively theatrical. I like the wide lip of the common foxglove's flowers and the way the blooms hang down like bells that might ring loudly at church. A favorite of mine, which is truly a plant for the discriminating gardener and one that definitely behaves as an annual in the West, is *D.* x *mertonensis*. A cross between *D. purpurea* and *D. grandiflora*, this form was cultivated in England at the John Innes Horticultural Institute, then at Merton, Surrey, in England, hence the species name. It is a stalwart plant, almost two feet high. The scooplike, rosy-mauve flowers, with hints of copper shading, are large and plentiful along the statuesque stems. These supercharged summer-blooming flowers are major attention-grabbers placed just a few feet from my front door.

An unusual form of digitalis, in name as well as in appearance, is *D. obscura*. The species name most definitely describes this flower; it is not well known to many gardeners. Unlike most foxgloves, this twelve-inch species, a native of Spain, likes full sun, although it will do well in partial shade. The tubular flowers are orange-yellow to brownish red. A few of these plants, with their uncommon coloring and flower shape, are delightful grouped together toward the front of a sunny or lightly shaded border. I am also fond of their narrow, green, swirly looking foliage. In a sunny site I have *D. obscura* paired with *Rosa blanda*, a species rose from eastern and central North America that has clustered, single pink flowers in spring. Close by these two plants is *Chrysanthemum weyrichii* 'White Bomb', which grows to about ten inches. From late summer into fall this mum is loaded with small white daisies. Be careful where you place it—it can be counted on to spread quickly in the garden.

Other forms of digitalis that are appropriate for partially shady sites are *D. lutea* (straw foxglove) and *D. lanata* (Grecian foxglove). Both of these species have erect yet slender stems. *D. lanata* has white or yellowish one-inch flowers with touches of brown and purple inside. The flowers are smaller than those of the common foxglove. *D. lutea* has more yellow coloring and is utterly graceful in appearance, as the stems sway in any breeze. Massed together, they are artistically dazzling. Situated close to this digitalis is *Echium vulgare* (viper's bugloss), a sun-loving flower that, in my experience, accepts some shade. A relative of the common herb borage, it is a reseeding annual. It can reach two feet or more with moisture, or it can withstand drought conditions and poor soil, remaining petite at about ten inches. Blooming in early summer, these plants have many half-inch tubular violet-blue flowers, flecked with white, running up and down the stalks. Sometimes the flowers of *Echium vulgare* can be pink or white. There are over a dozen stalks to each plant, and the foliage is narrow, hairy, and gray-green. Its simple, flat, twelve-inch dull-green rosette, which is fairly insignificant, gives no indication of the distinctive traits that burst forth weeks later in the summer. I have heard this plant described as "overly friendly," but it took six years to get established in my garden. Even if it eventually begins to gallop across my landscape, I consider myself fortunate to have it. These are impressive flowers when planted next to the creamy blooms of *Digitalis lutea*. There are a handful of other colorful species of *Echium* that I know to be cold-hardy in the West, and if I ever come across them, they will be in my garden in a flash!

On the outskirts of my shady garden I planted *Digitalis ferruginea* (rusty foxglove), known for its missilelike flowers that reach about three feet. This foxglove is planted at the edge of a raised garden bed, with the shrub rose 'Alba Semiplena' in the background. The flower color is a mix of yellow and brown. After its blooming cycle is complete, toward the end of summer, the twelve-inch-wide semi-evergreen rosettes continue to be attractive, with many six-inch-long leaves pressed to the ground. I leave the sturdy stalks standing in the fall, since the chocolate-brown seed capsules, cloaked in light green, add another phase of intrigue to the landscape. Depending on my mood, sometimes I will cut off the stiff yet attractive brownish red seedheads and make them into a bouquet for my coffee table, mixing them with other alluring seedheads of fall, including ornamental grasses, rose hips, and tall penstemons. When snows ravage the garden, turning this plant and others to mush, I finally clip what is left of the stems to the ground until they surge up again in spring.

In your shade garden, be bold in combining vertical and pillowlike forms. Mix them together in whatever style strikes your fancy. Pretend you are concocting your favorite luscious cake, and see what yummy flavor evolves in your garden, as you metaphorically shake in this spice (cushion plant) and that one (tall variety). By season's end, you will discover combinations that will thrill you. Experimentation unlocks a wealth of riches!

Low and Lovely

Two outstanding plants that I have woven throughout parts of my small front garden are *Corydalis ochroleuca* and *Lamium maculatum* 'White Nancy' (dead nettle). *C. ochroleuca* is low, under ten inches, with greenish-white flowers. It is related to the Colorado native *C. aurea*, whose flowers have a stronger yellow color. For many years I have let the greenish-white form, with its delicate, lacy-textured foliage, meander among various

The blotched groundcover *Lamium maculatum* 'White Nancy' (dead nettle) lies side by side with the early blooming yellow flowerheads of *Doronicum orientale* (leopard's bane).

Lamium maculatum 'White Nancy' (dead nettle) is dressed with a smattering of fallen leaves from an unknown plum tree. Bordering this bed is the lacy foliage of *Santolina rosmarinifolia* (green santolina cotton). A contented stone cat snuggles among the plants.

perennials. It blooms almost continually from late spring into fall, stifling weeds wherever it is planted and ensuring that this shaded garden needs minimal attention. Moreover, it makes a great companion plant to the spiky flowers of the digitalis that I grow here. I would not put it into a small rock garden because of its aggressive nature, but in a shady location it gently travels about, not being overly sociable to its neighbors. This plant was discovered in Italy in 1594. An oldster like my antique white rose, 'Alba Semiplena', which has persisted from the times of the Greeks and Romans, this groundcover was growing during the Renaissance when the alchemists were still stirring their brews. Now this plant is doing its magical stuff in my garden!

Lamium maculatum 'White Nancy' is the other groundcover that fills in around perennials in my shade garden. About the same height as the corydalis, it has variegated green and white foliage. The flowers are puffy white, rising four inches or so above the foliage. It is a vigorous grower but has not been invasive for me; when it travels where it is unwelcome, it is easily pulled up. I have three or four patches around my cottonwood tree and also near paths, where it makes a good edging plant.

Adjacent to these groundcovers is the reliable perennial *Knautia macedonica*. It has a bushy form and grows to about three feet. The flowerheads, a nice dark crimson, are one to two inches across and resemble the pincushion you are likely to find in grandmother's sewing kit. Knautias perform well in this east-facing garden, which gets only morning sun, although they easily adapt to full sun. After a few years, as the mother plant matures, I notice offshoots popping up nearby. As they develop, I dig up these young plants in early spring and move them to my back garden, where I have sun aplenty. I plant the knautia intuitively wherever I want this deep red color, which is not all that abundant in border flowers. To my surprise, knautia will even produce a few more flowers after a few inches of snow.

When I first began my front shade garden, I had a hunch I needed a few shrubs, but not too many. Four turned out to be just right. In one spot I planted an unfamiliar groundcover shrub, *Cotoneaster salicifolius* (willowleaf cotoneaster), which has become invaluable. Like other cotoneasters, this prostrate, usually evergreen shrub adapts quite well to various garden soils and situations, thriving either in a sandy or clayey mixture. It has been slowly creeping over my bare earth, filling in nicely, for the past five years. Its wide-spreading, arching branches extend to three feet, with small, glossy, dark green leaves. Over time it will be an excellent weed inhibitor as new tentacles dig into the soil, take root, and continue to stretch out further. I have not seen any signs of the scarlet berries it is reputed to have, but I'm sure they will come with age.

To create a dynamic duo, I have planted a few specimens of *Bergenia cordifolia* (heart-leaf Bergenia). In a shady site with adequate moisture, bergenias are excellent plants to group together, creating bold accents with their leathery, ladle-sized paddles of rich green. The spring-blooming mauve-pink flowers enhance the plant's appearance. True to its common name, it squeals like a pig when the leaves are gently rubbed between your fingers! The large, impressive foliage pressed closely against the miniature leaves of the cotoneaster creates a highly satisfactory contrast. Added zip to complete the picture comes again from

Lamium maculatum 'White Nancy', a stimulating and refreshing addition that lights up this shady area. For even more punch with textures and shapes, try the wide selection of hardy geraniums. Low ones such as *Geranium cinereum* var. *subcaulescens* and *G. renardii*, with their mounding habits, pair up well against the prominent, round leaves of the bergenias. *G. cinereum* var. *subcaulescens* is covered with vibrant, deep red flowers with a blackish eye. *G. renardii* has soft, sage-green, wrinkled leaves that are somewhat velvety in texture. The summer flowers are opal white with pronounced purple veins. It doesn't flower profusely, but I savor its distinctive foliage. It would also look great in a rock garden, as long as it received some protection against hot afternoon sun.

Poppies in Shade?

Most poppies prefer full sun, and all of mine thrive and perform beautifully in these ideal conditions. However, I have had success growing a few in partial shade. Like many gardeners, I like to wiggle into new territory and proclaim sweet success when the odds seem against me. Many factors, including plant placement, soil, microclimate, and occasional luck can lead to triumphant results. This has happened to me with two different poppies. The first is a little-known species called *Papaver dubium* (long-headed poppy). Its common name comes from its seed capsule, which is narrow and an inch or so long. The long-headed poppy is related to the reseeding annual *P. rhoea*s, or Shirley poppy, which comes in shades of red, pink, and white. Through the Denver Botanic Gardens, I obtained seed of *P. dubium*, which I casually scattered in my sunny backyard garden one fall. Within a few years, my garden was radiant with quarter-sized, slightly cupped, pink-red flowers dotted with tiny protruding green eyes. Not only did it bloom in spring with uncontrolled splendor in this area, but within a short time winds and birds had moved the seeds to my front garden, which is quite close to my house and receives only a few hours of sun. I was overjoyed, since this poppy has a preference for hot, dry Mediterranean conditions. It is also known as *P. modestum*, denoting its modest flower size, which is smaller than that of the Shirley poppy. The rosette of *P. dubium* can spread a foot across, with many strongly lobed leaves and wiry stems up to two feet high, covered with tiny silvery hairs.

Another poppy that traveled from my back to my front garden is *P. somniferum* (opium poppy). Although it blooms prolifically, it settled in a little farther away from my house and the cottonwood tree, where it receives more sun. The large (to four inches), flamboyant blooms of this poppy come in many colorful hues, including purple, pink, salmon, and red. Their petals overlap and bend, giving them a casual, nonchalant look. The erect stems, to

In fall, *Tovara virginiana* 'Painters Palette' exposes its thin red lines as it appears to be fenced in by
Corydalis ochroleuca on the left and the glimmering white flowers and variegated foliage
of *Lamium maculatum* 'White Nancy' (dead nettle).

approximately three feet, produce frilly leaves that are bluish or grayish green. The large, smooth, marble-shaped seed capsules are eye-catching in late summer after the flowers have finished their intense few weeks of bloom. Once the capsules turn beige, shake them and enjoy the sounds they make as the copious seeds jingle in the shells. By simply tearing off the tops of the shells, you can easily harvest the tiny dark-brown seeds, which is why I freely give so many away when I teach.

A few years back, Lauren Springer, author of *The Undaunted Gardener*, generously gave me seed of *P. somniferum* 'Lauren's Grape', so now I am delighted with this deep purple variety. Next to it is another backyard transplant, *Consolida ambigua* (larkspur), which looks lovely with its delicate blue spires of bloom reaching to two feet in this lightly shaded spot. Although the larkspur comes in other shades, such as lilac and white, the blue one predominates in my garden. I let both of these reseeding annuals emerge wherever I think they will look attractive. If too many appear for my taste, I easily eliminate the seedlings early in the season, or cut the seedheads off immediately after the plants have flowered. However, my gardening practices are not too controlling, as many plants interweave extensively, as though an abstract painter had created exquisite and colorful canvases.

A plant that I purposely planted in this partially shaded garden was *Filipendula vulgaris* (meadowsweet). I do not have very many of them because my shade garden is not extensive and my first loves for shade are hellebores, foxgloves, geraniums, and pulmonarias. When a colleague moved to a sunnier site, she passed this plant on to me, knowing that I would give it a good home with lots of tender loving care. It may be common, as its species name suggests, but its sprays of white flowers refresh any shady garden. When it blooms in early

The low-key blue flowers of *Nigella damascena* (love-in-a-mist) and its intricate foliage appear a perfect match when bonded next to *Oxalis crassipes* 'Rubra' (wood sorrel).

Photograph by John Davenport

summer, I also enjoy its low ferny green foliage, which has impact in the garden long after the flowers have disappeared. I planted it years ago, and shortly thereafter *Papaver somniferum* and *Consolida ambigua* decided to move in. Suddenly I realized that my garden had become patriotic, with red, white, and blue flowers!

In most cases I like it when plants move around and change homes in my garden. As they shift from one spot to another, they bring in visually stimulating ideas that I might not have been aware of. As plants multiply, I love to dig them up on a whim and move them wherever I imagine they will appeal to my senses. This approach reminds me of a phrase from my psychology background, "controlled abandon." This paradoxical concept fits my lighthearted gardening style. Some control is needed in gardening; otherwise, the garden is a mass of weeds with touches of color and texture. But I also like the carefree and open spirit that abandonment brings to the garden. At its foundation, this belief system is an alchemical union of opposites. One point of view, be it control or abandon, is not better than the other. Both are mighty contributors to the overall scheme in my garden.

Trial and Error in the Shade

Knowing that geraniums are high-performance plants in partially shady locations, I tried a new one a few years ago. Because a colleague was going to a plant sale that I was unable to attend, I asked her to pick up anything unique and wonderful. She bought a geranium whose tag said it had purplish pink flowers. I was thrilled with this cute plant, which was supposed to bloom from spring into fall! But alas, for me, *Geranium pyrenaicum* (mountain cranesbill) was not a wonderful specimen. One book I read said it grew very quickly. What an understatement! *G. pyrenaicum* is highly prolific; in fact, I would call it a major weed. That first spring it looked wonderful, with its low, lax habit, as it bloomed in front of the taller *Papaver dubium*, and the red flowers of the poppy and the purplish pink of the geranium made a great combination. But a divorce was imminent. When fall arrived, I needed to rip it all out. It had become a serious nuisance as it ravenously crept into the small amount of grass circling my cottonwood; it also sped through my other flowerbeds. A few years later, I continue to pull it out here and there; I devoutly hope that in a short time I will not see a trace of it.

Another shade plant that I definitely researched too late was *Carex lanuginosa*. One cool late-fall day I had time on my hands, so impulsively I went to prowl a nursery. My eyes were drawn to this darling, short, grasslike plant. Ornamental grasses of any kind are a passion of mine, so this sedge piqued my interest. The tag warned of its aggressive nature, but I ignored it and purchased it anyway. It moved quickly throughout my garden, getting a little too comfortable wherever it landed, especially in the moister spots. Again, here was a plant that simply had to go.

Though I make mistakes now and then and put in a plant that is not appropriate to the site, my view is that gardening is not extremely technical, and that I'm not performing a serious surgical procedure. If something goes in the wrong spot, it can be removed or changed or adjusted somehow. I enjoy being adventuresome and relying on my hunches—the wrong turn can easily be corrected, and the good surprises are well worth a few small errors.

Lingering in the Shade

I'm thrilled with plants that bloom late in fall, around the time of our first snowfall, which usually appears toward the end of September. When I plan my shade garden I look for long-blooming, unusual plants with contrast potential. A distinctive and sometimes hard-to-come-by perennial that meets all these criteria is *Persicaria virginiana* 'Painter's Palette' (also known as *Tovara virginiana* 'Painter's Palette'). This three-by-three-foot perennial is prized for two attributes: its outstanding foliage and its wandlike flowers. Toward the end of summer, it appears as if an artist has snuck into my garden and, unbeknownst to me, has splashed the two-inch-wide leaves with cream, yellow, and dabs of pink and chocolate-colored paint. How spectacular! For two months, as summer rolls into fall, this specimen is one of the highlights in this area. Toward the end of September—and beyond, if the weather behaves itself—thin, dazzling-red, wavy wands appear, growing eight inches out of the strongly marked foliage. *P. virginiana* 'Painter's Palette' is quite a thirsty plant, speaking up with drooping leaves when it wants a drink of water. Because of its many exceptional features I have strategically planted it here and there around the cottonwood, where it adds grace and elegance as autumn leaves begin to gently drift to the ground.

To contrast with such a gorgeous plant, I was again, as often happens in spring and summer, browsing a nearby nursery when I saw something new and titillating: *Oxalis crassipes* 'Rosea'. While some forms of oxalis are weedy, such as the well-known *O. corniculata* (wood sorrel or clover), with its explosive seedpods that scatter seeds more than ten feet away when mature, I have had much more success with this oxalis than I had with the geranium and the carex discussed above. This plant has petite, heart-shaped leaves, thinner than paper, that come three to a stem. The showy rose-pink flowers of this low, compact plant begin blooming midspring. Flower production keeps chugging along, taking a few breaks in the summer, but still producing color into October, even after a few minor

MUCH ADO ABOUT MULCH

Among avid gardeners, mulch can be a hotly debated topic, with some strong and varied opinions. Most rock gardeners favor rock mulch to "dress" their rock gardens. They put a few inches all around their cute little plants (or their larger-sized ones). This acts as a weed barrier, looks attractive, keeps the plants from drying out, and—quite critical to the effect— mimics the look of high mountain ranges in the Alps and other mountainous regions around the world. Very subjectively, the gardener chooses color and size of stone mulch to match the décor of his or her garden. Some folks are fussy and consider their rock choice critical to the design of their garden, while others will make do. I'm a make-doer. I have pea-sized stone mulch all over my rock gardens, as well as on many of my paths. Once it compacts, after a few months, it's comfortable to walk on, and I like the way it looks among my rock garden plants. Other gardeners may prefer larger sizes of stone, and some even like to make a mixture of different sizes and colors.

Rock mulch can also be used appropriately for various styles of flower beds, especially where the owner wants to limit the use of water. Any area where mowing grass is difficult, or where the terrain is hilly or hoses won't reach, can be transformed into a so-called dry garden, which would look very attractive with stone mulch.

Controversy also swirls around wood mulch. (I define "wood mulch" as any kind of woody material that can be shoveled or spread among plants.) Again, the range of choices is quite broad. A gardener can choose to use larger pieces of wood, or shredded bark or very fine pieces of wood, or anything in between. All wood mulch will eventually break down, enriching the soil and benefiting the plants. However, larger pieces will take much longer to break down.

Late fall is an excellent time to surround your perennials and shrubs with mulch, which will protect them from the ravages of Old Man Winter and feed the plants for future seasons. A good compost mixture, too, will do the trick. In late fall or early spring, I often put down a few inches of rich organic matter all through my flower beds. I don't do my rock garden, which would be an almost impossibly time-consuming task.

If any spot is appropriate for wood mulch, it is a shady woodland garden. Shade gardens seem to have an especially natural feeling, which wood mulches complement nicely. Trees, whether multistemmed or single-trunked, fit in naturally with wood mulch. The combination brings to mind the mountains, with their rugged terrain, humus-rich soils and, below timberline, abundance of trees.

If your life is busy and tightly scheduled, barely affording you time to put a few plants in, let alone do the weeding, then by all means go for wood mulch. Wood mulch has many benefits: It gives the garden an attractive appearance; it keeps the soil cool, reducing cracking and drying out when the weather is blistering hot; and it inhibits weeds.

If you are a casual gardener who pokes in a few annuals and perennials every year, mulch may be an asset to you. You could spend less time in the garden, affording you more time to attend to other hobbies or to work. Let's say you are a young mom with toddlers scrambling at your knees. Would gardening be fun and relaxing for you? You may love it, but you might struggle to find the time. Use mulch, deal with the kids, and putter in the garden on weekends or when you have a babysitter. Or let the kids dig in the dirt too!

Whether or not you mulch depends also on your tolerance for weeds. Some people are fussier than others—weeds really bother them. Others barely see weeds, or don't care until they become uncontrollable. A thick layer of mulch can definitely help with general weed control.

There is a certain category of passionate gardeners to which I belong. I am consumed by my passion, never missing a chance to check out the latest arrivals at local garden centers. I rarely pass up the opportunity to browse the garden section at our local bookstore as well, even though I can barely fit more books on my shelves. The librarian at the Denver Botanic Gardens once observed, when I complained that I had no room for more books, that it was time to weed my bookshelves! I garden constantly. Some gardeners, like myself, who can always squeeze gardening into our day and call it heaven, do not feel the necessity to mulch. We plant thickly, meaning that we plant our flowers fairly close to each other, so as they mature and fill in, they act as the protective mulch, cooling the soil and inhibiting weeds.

The dense planting approach is not a totally new concept; it is a wave that has surfaced again. Amateur horticulturists in the late 1800s were encouraged to cultivate plants and write books about their personal experiences. One such author was poet and essayist Celia Thaxter, who wrote *Island Garden* in 1894. Her garden was located on the windswept island of Appledore, near Portsmouth, New Hampshire. As Yvonne Cuthbertson points out in *Women Gardeners*, Thaxter too was an advocate of dense planting, insisting that every piece of ground be covered with flowers so that there would be continuous and stunning blooms. Another viewpoint is that mulch can sometimes be used temporarily as the plants fill in. This approach saves on the task of weeding, yet the plants gradually grow and spread, and the mulch seems to disappear underneath them.

If using wood mulch is your choice, for an attractive appearance I suggest small pieces. The large two-inch sizes look bulky and unnatural and seem to take forever to break down. Be careful not to spread the mulch on too thick. Two or three inches is more than enough to do the job. Too much mulch will inhibit the growth and performance of your plants. Also, with too thick a layer of mulch you are creating spots that might be more prone to pests and diseases, especially if the area gets extra moisture.

There is no right or wrong answer to the dilemma of whether to mulch or not. Each person has a different lifestyle and a different type of garden, which he or she needs to evaluate individually. Like so many decisions in the garden, mulching is a matter of personal choice. ■

snowfalls. If you prefer a white-flowered form, try *Oxalis crassipes* 'Alba'—and if Latin is not your cup of tea, just ask for "white strawberry oxalis."

To make a contrast with the delicate foliage of this flower, nearby I've planted a dwarf pine that is content in partial shade. After six years, *Pinus strobus* 'Blue Shag' has grown to three feet, with branches stretching out almost as far. The soft, two-inch-long needles almost beg to be caressed (unlike those of spruces, whose sharp and pointed needles make people, especially children, hesitant to approach and touch).

I like having plants that are tempting to touch as well as to sniff and see in my garden. Plants that offer a smorgasbord of possibilities stretch the garden into new dimensions and bring people closer to nature. When visitors come through my garden, I often offer them pieces of various plants to look at more closely, so they can examine the foliage, seeds, and definitely the scent. Their facial expressions are fascinating to watch as they reveal their preferences for various scents. With small groups, I enjoy sharing many of the seeds that I have gathered from my garden. Fellow gardeners are always delighted to receive free packages of seeds, particularly after they have seen the flower in bloom or if they have been admiring it in books or at nurseries but have not gotten around to purchasing it.

A shrub that I would not be without is *Daphne* x *burkwoodii* 'Carol Mackie'. Landscapers and garden designers have been using this shrub extensively over the last ten years, and in our region it is considered a star performer for partially shaded sites. Because of its adaptability and hardiness in the West, it was named Plant Select®. (Plant Select is a program administered by the Denver Botanic Gardens and Colorado State University along with landscapers and nursery professionals to introduce new or underused plants to the Rocky Mountain region.) This variegated, sometimes-evergreen shrub, which I planted near my front entrance, has one-inch leaves etched with pale creamy yellow markings. It helps frame my entryway, adding structure throughout the year; except in the coldest of winters, it stays evergreen. In early spring it boasts small pink blossoms with a heady, delicious fragrance that wafts through this small shady enclosure.

Another popular plant that I've used frequently is *Ceratostigma plumbaginoides* (leadwort). This low-mounding groundcover is excellent for partially shaded sites. The soupspoon-shaped foliage of the leadwort turns shades of bronzy red, and its dainty blue flower will continue to bloom through a few of our early snows. Red is a powerful color as it works its magic in the fall.

To discover which shade plants linger on in fall or add winter structure with attractive foliage, I've done my share of experimenting. I randomly buy whatever appeals to me, with the goal of obtaining a fair number of plants whose foliage and flowers have distinctive traits, such as nice fall color, unusual flowers, or eye-catching texture. I rely on my intuition as to how to group these different plants. For instance, I like unusual evergreens, rather than the more familiar spruces and junipers. From the eastern portion of the United States, I have used *Paxistima canbyi* (mountain lover). This dense shrub, which has tiny dark green leaves, grows slowly to reach about one foot. Because of its tiny leaves, I place it near bergenias, with their large, deep reddish winter foliage, or near hellebores, whose foliage is also large and evergreen. All three of these plants add diversity and appeal to the shade garden in cooler months.

In one client's garden, I used *Lamium maculatum* 'White Nancy' in a shady site. The planting was beneath some plum trees; in late fall, the richly colored purple leaves from the tree fell on the 'White Nancy', accidentally creating a pleasing picture.

I like to think of my garden as a sort of Garden of Eden, where my imagination and intuition get fired up with what I see before me. And without a shade garden it would not be complete. I'm always delighted when I come up with a new plant that will enhance a quiet, shady site where I can place a bench, grab a cool drink, and relax for a moment. If your property has what seems like an overabundance of trees, don't be discouraged. Look at your shady sites as opportunities for creativity, where you can express yourself with a palette of many plants that offer tempting textures, forms, colors, and sizes.

The tan plumage of *Calamagrostis acutiflora* 'Karl Foerster' (feather reed grass) makes a nice background accent with the purple flowers of *Eryngium planum* (sea holly), the yellow blossoms of *Heliopsis helianthoides* (sunflower heliopsis), as well as the low-bending foliage of *Bromus benekenii* (brome grass).

CHAPTER FIVE

Gorgeous Grasses Fly in the Breeze

Historical Background

Grasses cover the earth, blanketing almost one-fifth of the world's land area. Grass was one of the first plants to evolve, and humans have had a long relationship with grasses. In fact, according to *The Encyclopedia of Ornamental Grasses* by John Greenlee, our ancestors are believed to have evolved in the grasslands of Africa. The human diet is connected to the grass family in many instances. Edible grains such as wheat, barley, rice, and rye are staples for many peoples of the world. The grass *Saccharum*

Above: A lovely path border of maiden grass, coneflower, and many other flowers.

officinarum (sugar cane), which originated in tropical Southeast Asia, has been cultivated for centuries and sweetens much of the food we consume. Other members of the grass family, including some species of *Panicum* (switch grass), *Festuca* (fescue), and *Bouteloua gracilis* (blue gramma) provide forage for livestock. In many cultures grasses are woven into hats, mats, roofs, and fences.

Grasses exist throughout North America and the world in wetlands and on both dry and moist prairies, where there once was an abundance of diversity in the grass kingdom. But alas, in the name of progress and movement of the plow, much of this natural and beautiful habitat has been eliminated or is painfully dwindling. As more of the American landscape is taken over by malls, houses, and highways, grasses are threatened with extinction.

However, along with the loss of grassland, over approximately the last one hundred and fifty years ornamental grasses have come to be valued more highly by gardeners. "Ornamental" is the key word here. Just like trees, shrubs, and other plant material, grasses are living ornaments. They stimulate any landscape with their exuberance and fullness. The "ornamental" label is applied not only to true grasses but to grasslike plants in general. True grasses are members of the family Gramineae (sometimes called Poaceae), but in this chapter I also look at the genus *Ophiopogon* (mondo grasses, which actually belong to the lily family) and at the family known as Cyperaceae (sedges) because these two groups of grasslike plants have leaf structure and color that work in the garden much like the ornamental grasses, adding new elegance and style to our landscapes. In addition, I finally examine the genus *Juncaceae*, the rushes, to which *Luzula* belongs. (Of course, turf grass will always have its place for recreation and enjoyment, but as we grow more ecologically aware and realize that water is a limited natural resource, we will increasingly plant alternatives to thirsty bluegrass.)

In regard to grasses, I nod my head in agreement when I read what Clarence Elliott, a popular nurseryman, wrote in 1935. The following statement applied mainly to grasses in the rock garden; however, I believe it can be adapted to practically any style of flower bed. In *Rock Garden Plants*, he wrote, "Grasses are a corrective to the temptation to have flowers, flowers, flowers, and colour, over every inch of the rock garden." Another well-known horticulturist and gardener, Graham Stuart Thomas, notes in his book *The Rock Garden and Its Plants* that grasslike foliage is necessary in the garden for relief. It creates balance, bringing in a perspective that has been ignored for too long. The effect of grasses comes from their unique repetition of curving lines. If we add to this feature the floral display of the plumes and the color offered by the foliage, their value is enormously upgraded. How do grasses enhance the garden? Let me count the ways! Do I want drama, texture, and height? Ornamental grasses distinctly provide these qualities. Design-wise, try them near or behind any large rocks or boulders. Tremendous contrast emerges between the airy, light, loosely branching flower clusters (panicles) of grasses and the denseness and shape of the stone. Grasses present unique structure, color, and vertical interest. In addition, many varieties come to life when wind moves through the blades, thus bringing an entirely new quality into the garden: motion.

Given the great variety of choices, the gardener can have an attractive grass for any situation. There are grasses for groundcover, edging beds, screening, and accent. The range of grasses for use on our home sites is much wider than the knowledge most of us have about how to use them artistically in our gardens. There are spreading grasses, clumping grasses, those for wet or dry sites, for sun or part shade. Grasses successfully rise to any challenge, no matter what style of garden you have. They may be upright or arching, in tight tufts or displaying an open habit. Their heights range from about six inches for alpine varieties such the Colorado native *Festuca brachyphylla*, which I planted a few years ago, with its diminutive silvery green plumes in spring and a mingling of maroon and buff colors in fall, to the bold *Arundo donax* (giant reed). According to Carole Ottesen, author of *Ornamental Grasses: The Amber Wave*, this grass is thought to have been the first grass intentionally brought to the New World. Transplanted to California by the Spanish mission fathers, it was made into animal pens, woven into baskets, and grown for protection from the wind. This mammoth plant will reach huge proportions—ten to fifteen feet, even for gardeners in cold regions, depending on the amount of sun and moisture it receives, as well as its location. The thick foliage is colored gray, green, and blue, with foot-long beige flowers. This plant has dramatic architectural qualities; use it near the water's edge, where its stems can arch over the bank and be reflected in the water. I have also seen it used effectively at a zoo, where it acts as a tree, dominating a specific area viewed by visitors, but not too close to hungry giraffes or other tall animals! Obviously, it is only for those gardeners who have the space for it.

Many grasses not only look swanky but harmonize extremely well when mixed with other plant material. Landscapers and garden designers have noted this complementary quality, inspiring a general surge of interest in ornamental grasses. Grasses have a life cycle that changes month by month and day by day. Compared to more traditional plants, they don't need much clipping, staking, or deadheading. Once they are established you can just leave them alone, except for the annual ritual of cutting them back. (Toward the end of this chapter I'll describe how easy it is to care for these grasses.)

At various times in our nation's history, ornamental grasses have moved back and forth from being in favor, as they are now, to near obscurity. In seed books and catalogs during

The glistening foliage of *Stipa comata* (needle and thread grass) droops among
the stones and *Salvia sclarea* (clary sage). Off to the right is *Crambe cordifolia* (giant kale).

the late 1800s and the early part of the twentieth century, there were numerous references
to ornamental grasses. Companies were selling packets of seed for only five or ten cents. In
the John Gardiner and Company (Philadelphia) Seed Annual for 1890, the category for
"Grasses (ornamental)" lists fifteen different possibilities. Included are *Stipa pennata*
(feather grass), an English native also listed among flowering plants in a seed catalog from
1782; *Arundo donax*; and *Eulalia* (now called *Miscanthus sinensis*).

In the 1930s, Wayside Gardens of Mentor, Ohio, began selling grasses such as *Saccharum
ravennae* (plume grass or hardy pampas grass), *Pennisetum alopecuroides* (fountain grass), and
Phalaris arundinacea var. *picta* (ribbon grass or gardener's garters). As a gardener, I was
attracted to the variegated, silky-smooth greenery of ribbon grass and planted some in my
garden. If I had let it continue, it would have overtaken my suburban neighborhood with no
effort! For a few years, when I saw its foliage emerge, I constantly hacked away at it,
reaching deep below the roots. As a local company, Alameda Wholesale Nursery, says in its
2000 catalog, "Very invasive, spreads like butter on a hot summer day." To its credit, I have

seen ribbon grass used beautifully in a strictly controlled environment, surrounded by rocks or concrete, which act as a barrier to prevent it from swimming too close to other plants. I have also seen it boost a planting when it encompassed a mature tree. The soft, low, green-and-white blades, which catch the wind, are the antithesis of the solid bark of the trunk.

By the 1940s, ornamental grasses were sinking in popularity in the United States. The immaculate, manicured, bright green lawn became a staple in suburbia. The use of Kentucky bluegrass quickly spread throughout the country, and people still pour millions of dollars' worth of chemicals and money onto their yards in search of the "perfect" lawn.

In spite of the high rank bluegrass gained during this period, some folks still paid attention to their surroundings, noticing miles upon miles of open prairie with its wavy attractive grasses. Again in Carole Ottesen's book *Ornamental Grasses: The Amber Wave*, the first large-scale restoration of a Midwestern prairie was undertaken in the 1930s at the University of Wisconsin. Soon other universities, nature centers, and wildlife refuges were collecting and planting seeds to establish their own prairies. The steamrolling energy to add grasses to our landscapes was beginning. Prairie Nursery, which opened in 1972 in Westfield, Wisconsin, wanted to promote grasses and natives. Neil Diboll, an expert on native grasses and wildflowers, took over the business in 1982 and has continued the focus on these plants. He has been a pioneer in his field, selling appropriate seed mixtures for homeowners and professional landscapers.

Slowly homeowners are discovering alternatives to bluegrass. This is happening in part through classes at garden centers and botanic gardens. Also, as homeowners see grasses displayed at garden centers and institutions around town, they become curious about these different plants and want to purchase them to complement their abundant flowers. As nurserymen hear the call for grasses from customers, they relay this need to larger distributors who sell grasses to garden centers. The public is eager to learn how to use this unfamiliar plant material. A homeowner may ask, "Where do I put a ten-foot grass?" Or, "How far apart do I plant *Miscanthus sinensis* 'Yaku Jima'?" Or, most typically, "What does the flower of this grass look like?" Some salespeople know, while others are greenhorns in the realm of grasses. Often, customers and nursery salespeople are attending the same classes and sharing information about these plants.

An important point to note is that most grasses appear pretty unattractive at a garden center. The beginning gardener sees only puny sticks or apparently dead foliage in a grouping of black pots. Unless you are a knowledgeable gardener, why would you be attracted to such plants? Obviously, you wouldn't. At least, with other perennials, you can often be drawn to their color and shape. Unless a knowledgeable person is helping where grasses are being sold, most people stay away from them, and thus sales are low.

Ornamental grasses have remained popular in Europe from the 1930s to this day. A pioneering nurseryman, Karl Foerster (1874–1970), was instrumental in developing a more naturalistic style of garden design. He based his ideas on nursery experiments and his observation of grasses growing in association with other plants in their native habitat. In 1957 he published *Using Grasses and Ferns in the Garden*, and in a catalog of his from the 1940s he lists over a hundred types of ornamental grasses. Foerster characterized grasses as "Mother Earth's hair" because they cover such a large portion of the earth. In recognition of his enormous contribution to grasses and to horticulture, *Calamagrostis* x *acutiflora* 'Karl Foerster' (feather reed grass) was named for him and can be seen, standing tall, throughout the gardens of the world. In fact, it was named Perennial Plant of the Year for 2001 by the Perennial Plant Association of America.

A premier plantsman who carries on the philosophy of Karl Foerster is Kurt Bluemel, who began his nursery business, Kurt Bluemel, Inc., in the mid-1960s in Maryland. His nursery propagates and promotes all forms of grasses nationwide, offering a huge selection of grasses and other plant material. It is also world famous for introducing new selections into the public eye as well as for educating people with videos, slides, and up-to-date book selections.

In terms of ornamental grasses, Americans were strongly influenced by two renowned English gardeners, William Robinson and Gertrude Jekyll. In 1889 William Robinson first published *The English Flower Garden*. For Robinson, the garden was a place in which unusual plants should be grown, with particular attention and the highest regard to their form, foliage, and color. (Sounds like the kind of garden many of us want now!) He believed these qualities should govern the design of the garden. About a North American native species that he liked, *Panicum virgatum* (switch grass), he wrote: "Admirable for borders or for isolation in the picturesque flower garden or pleasure ground. Its colour, though quiet, is pretty throughout the autumn, and not without effect even in the winter."

In an earlier book, *The Wild Garden*, published in 1870, Robinson spoke about his love of grass:

> *Except where wanted as a carpet, Grass may often be allowed to grow even in the pleasure ground; quite as good an effect is afforded by unmown as by mown Grass...indeed, better when the long Grass is full of flowers. Three-fourths of the most lovely flowers of cold and temperate regions are companions of the Grass...like Grasses in hardiness, like Grasses in summer life and winter rest, like Grasses in stature. Whatever plants may seem best to associate together in gardens, an immense number...more than two thousand species of those now cultivated...would thrive to perfection among our meadow Grasses, as they do on the Grassy breast of the mountain in many northern lands.*

Robinson refers to specific grasses, including *Chasmanthium latifolium* (northern sea oats). He also mentions *Carex pendula* (weeping sedge) for shady spots. I have been growing these two grasses for a number of years, although I had to obtain the sedge from a specialized nursery back East as recently as six years ago. With newer or rare cultivars, gardeners often have to go to extra lengths to locate a specimen. The sedge grows almost three feet high and, contrary to a few references, does not need continuously moist soil in order to strut its elongated nodding wheat-colored whips. In fact, keeping the soil somewhat dry helps keep this carex in check so that it does not spread too quickly, which it does not in my garden. Weeping sedge gives a spark to my front shady garden, visually softening the corky bark of my gigantic cottonwood tree.

Northern sea oats, the other grass William Robinson admired, is a favorite of mine because of its awesome panicles. These inflorescences develop in late summer and early fall. To a small degree they resemble teeth on a saw, but unlike saw teeth, these flowers are soft and papery thin. They give the grass a bouncy appearance, as if someone had attached a thin string to the flowers and yanked on them, pulling them down. This grass has light green leaves that turn bronzy with the onset of fall. It prefers a rich and moderately moist location in partial shade, where it will increase slowly over time. (Sun is fine too, if you give this grass adequate moisture.) Use it as a specimen plant, or plant several together so that their intricate leaves can make a bold statement. I use this grass in my front garden, where it makes a wonderful interruption among the many shade-loving plants with different leaf patterns and flower colors. Among the plants I unintentionally scattered near three of these grasses is *Aconitum* 'Spark's Variety' (monkshood), growing to three feet in my garden, with its one-inch-long, bluish purple flowers and large talonlike leaves. In this area too is x *Heucherella alba* 'Rosalie', which grows to just over a foot with dark green, blotchy, triangular leaves, topped off with short pink-flowered spires. Along the edge of this bed a small-leafed white geranium makes a tidy mound.

Gertrude Jekyll also used geraniums in her planting schemes because of their adaptability in shady sites. She was well known for her bold gardening style, and seemed to appreciate the "wildness" of William Robinson's plantings. Grasses mentioned in her works include some of those recorded by Robinson, such as *Arundo donax* (giant reed) and *Leymus arenarius* (wild rye). She used the latter in her gray garden border, and I'm personally familiar with it: Years ago, because of my naïveté in the realm of gardening, I bought this grass, or the American form of it. I meant it to grow along an edge, but it quickly became a large plot! Luckily, I removed it as soon as I became aware of its nasty invasive behavior. Gardeners who want this blue color should use instead *Helictotrichon sempervirens* (blue oat grass or blue avena grass), which stays put quite well wherever it is planted.

I don't follow any rules when it comes to adding grasses to my garden; I follow my internal murmurs and see where contrast would animate a particular site. For instance, if the spot has an abundance of roses or other globular flowers, then I'll imagine that grasses would add a lively thrust of diversity. The real beauty of a garden lies in how plants are combined, such as roses with grasses, or annuals with perennials. Grasses are a major contributor in this scenario. Their repetitive thin and wide lines, panicles, and varying heights and colors increase the aesthetic of any garden, and I encourage you to try a few grasses in your landscape.

My love for ornamental grasses began fifteen years ago as I browsed garden centers to check out perennials and began noticing these homely plants tucked away in corners. However, for me, they were fresh and new; I'm always willing to attempt something unfamiliar. If need be I did some research, but often I just bought and planted, taking a chance, discovering something new that would enhance my garden. Each time I was at the nursery I would be attracted to varieties that I had not heard of before. I snatched these up quickly. Luckily for me, their popularity had been slow to spread, so I usually had a fairly good selection to choose from. With only the slightest nod as to design, I knew generally to buy or group the grasses in my garden in clumps—that impacts the visual senses—of three or five or even seven. Sometimes just one would do the trick, because of its voluptuous size. I became consumed with ornamental grasses! Tall or short, any size, shape, or color was potential for my cart. My garden, adorned with more than seventy captivating grasses, would be sorely lacking in radiance without them.

Wind and Weaving

One of the major strengths of grasses is the striking way they can be woven among other plant material. Observing them as they wave calmly in the wind is soothing and restful to the soul. Sometimes, as I rush about my house, I'll take a minute and look out my window, while gusts of strong winds swirl the grasses about, disturbing their panicles. Because of their harmonious nature and diverse characteristics grasses are often showstoppers—without even asking to be! The reawakened passion for grasses brings a vast world of natural plant beauty into our gardens. As gardeners we are drawing on resources and ideas from fields, meadows, and mountains, creating beautiful spaces in which to enjoy outdoor activities or simply to stop, chat, and sip tea.

Speaking of restful spots, the patio is a good place to observe *Helictotrichon sempervirens*, with its fine, powdery blue foliage and extended beige plumes. An important feature to

On the far left, *Holcus mollis* 'Variegatus' (creeping soft grass) is caressed by the copious leaves of *Hosta sieboldiana* 'Frances Williams'. Overlapping the Hosta is the well-veined greenery of *Aruncus dioicus* (goatsbeard).

remember with this grass is spacing. If you are planting two or more, they need to be spaced at least three feet apart; otherwise, they will look too crowded, and the full effect of their expressive plumes will not be realized. To set off the beauty of the dramatic plumes and create a peekaboo effect, place colorful plants behind the cylindrical blades of this multi-use grass. This combination achieves a layering effect and brings in a new dimension.

I like being surprised as I walk my garden, encountering bright color and artistic images. Asiatic, trumpet, and Oriental lilies are excellent choices to be used with blue avena grass, since it is not extremely dense. The lilies, with their outgoing color range, which includes apricots, pinks, yellows, and copper tones, are delightful mates for a see-through effect. In front of this grass, and continuing the wave of color and interest, I like the moundy habit of *Coreopsis grandiflora* 'Baby Sun', whose yellow flowers can copy a lily of similar coloring. Nearby is *Veronica spicata* 'Blue Charm'. Its spikes of blue flowers mimic the grass because they both are tall and thin. The intense blue foliage of the grass is also similar to the lustrous green color of the leaves of the veronica. Providing a nice canopy for these plants is a small tree, *Acer tataricum* subsp. *ginnala* (Amur maple).

A plant that pairs up well with blue avena grass is *Allium caeruleum* (blue garlic), also known as *A. azureum*. The clear blue flowers sit balanced on tall, skinny stems. The blue color and round shape of the allium contrast beautifully against the grayish foliage and fanlike straight lines of the grass. To further accentuate the use of this bulb in a dryer spot in the garden, I suggest using it with silver plants such as *Artemisia* 'Powis Castle'. This combination is a marriage made in heaven! I like the way the detailed, intricate leaves of the artemisia play off the globular form of the alliums, and the way the blue of the allium flowers pairs nicely next to the silver-gray foliage of the artemisia.

In one of my perennial shrub borders, to create an effective textural arrangement as well as a feast for the eyes, I have used two different grasses along with shades of purple and blue. In summertime, I like the wave-in-the-wind appearance of *Calamagrostis* x *acutiflora* 'Karl Foerster'. Its pronounced vertical growth is a strong contrast to *Bromus benekenii* (brome grass). This shorter, pale tan grass, which may be difficult to find in garden centers, gracefully bends in front of its taller cousin, and another couple is bonded in matrimony. To perk up this picture I like *Eryngium planum* (sea holly), with its sharp, prickly, purplish flowers. The rounded, thistlelike flowerheads bring in another shape to contrast with the grasses. Growing nearby are blue veronicas, as well as a light lavender ornamental onion, *Allium senescens* (mountain or German garlic). Its cup-shaped flowers peer through the leaves of the bromus, creating a pleasant juxtaposition.

Because of its powerful presence, I have placed feather reed grass in several places around my garden. Unlike other large or wide-spreading grasses, this one is mighty yet undemanding in its space requirements. Since many flowers are circular, delicate, wide, or short, I have often used the projectile appearance of this grass to vary a planting scheme.

Another spectacular feather reed grass is *Calamagrostis brachytricha* (Korean feather reed grass). This species, which was discovered in Korea in the mid-1960s, differs in a few ways from *C.* x *acutiflora* 'Karl Foerster' and *C.* x *acutiflora* 'Overdam' (more about these two cultivars in Chapter Six). Both of these grasses have plumes that are fairly tapered and bloom in summer. *C. brachytricha*, with its half-inch-wide medium-green leaves, forms a small vaselike clump in summer. Because its leaves are thicker than those of many ornamental grasses, it adds a special effect. Then, almost instantaneously, the plant transforms and is chock full of fluffy flowers tinted a sultry rose-purple. For a contrasting foliage shape, I have again used *Eryngium planum*. An added member of this planting scheme is *Deschampsia caespitosa* (tufted hair grass). Although both grasses are cloaked in shades of sandy brown in fall, their silhouettes are strikingly different: Korean feather reed grass is fluffy-looking and robust, reminding me of narrow bunches of cotton candy, while the tufted hair grass is decorated with ethereal panicles and bends gently. For more flair with these two grasses, plant *Rudbeckia triloba* (black-eyed Susan); its almost-black seedheads in winter strike a powerful mark.

Deschampsia caespitosa is an appealing grass. This native is a common sight in the Rocky Mountains and throughout the Northern Hemisphere in meadows and somewhat moist areas. While hiking I have seen hilly meadows massed with hundreds of clumps of this grass. Rising many feet above its deep green and delicate foliage were scores of straight, green-and-cream-colored aspen trunks. On some trees the bark was dark-brown or gray, pockmarked by their advanced age. I was struck by the vast difference between these two plants; the green, airy grass coupled with the bulky, stout character of the aspen shooting skyward to the clouds. This grass grows well in partial shade when mixed with ferns and other shade-loving plants. However, it also adapts equally well to sun-soaked areas and prospers there if it gets adequate moisture.

An eye-catching cultivar of this species is *D. flexuosa* (crinkled hair grass). Its stems are thread-thin, and the bleached inflorescences are patterned like grain in a wheat field. Nearby in my garden is *Boltonia asteroides* 'Snowbank'. As I walk down my flagstone path, I like the airy effect I see when the effusive white daisies appear to dance with the panicles of the hair grass.

A dainty yet distinctive grass is *Stipa comata* (needle-and-thread grass). The over one hundred fifty species of *Stipa* boast some of the dressiest flowers one can find on a grass. Their threadlike structures catch light; the semi-transparent, silky awns sparkle vibrantly in morning and afternoon sunlight. Toward the tips of *S. comata*, some of the narrow feathery growth twists and curls, reminding me of an old man's beard and adding yet another attractive visual quality. This grass is adaptable, and I have had success with it whether the soil is dry or somewhat moist, but it seems to prefer good drainage. Over time it will increase, so I suggest monitoring its behavior. I have it planted on a steep slope where it hangs downward and mixes with *Salvia sclarea* (clary sage), with its pale lavender flowers. This sage generously self-sows, so I weed out most of the seedlings when they are small, letting a few remain because I enjoy the colorful flowers. Viewing these two plants together, I enjoy the straight, almost-white lines of the grass, in contrast to the purple blooms of the sage. Near these two smaller flowers I placed *Crambe cordifolia*. Because of its large size, I have heard gardeners refer to it as "baby's breath on steroids"!

In a sunny corner of my garden, surrounded by an easy-walk-around gravel path, I have brought together plants with similar characteristics, in addition to those with radically

Lysimachia ciliata (hairy loosestrife), with its dark foliage, bonds with my cottonwood tree as *Corydalis ochroleuca,* on the far left, shows off its mass of white flowers. The grasslike plant is *Luzula sylvatica* (woodrush).

opposed forms. *Echinops bannaticus* 'Taplow Blue' (globe thistle), with its intricate, piercingly blue flower, is a good companion when placed in back of *Deschampsia flexuosa.* The foliage of the globe thistle is prickly to the touch, contrasting with the smooth thin lines of the grass. In this area is *Alchemilla mollis* (lady's mantle). Although it needs division in early spring every two or three years, I find this to be an extremely versatile plant. Its fanlike foliage, lime-yellow flowers, and sprawling form make it a favorite choice for garden designers. I especially like to admire the plant after it has rained or when dew has settled on the leaves; the moisture looks like swollen rain drops and glistens when hit just right by the sunlight. Lady's mantle mixes well with an endless variety of shrubs and perennials.

Surround it with shrub roses, *Heuchera* (coral bells), and any plant with vivid red flowers. It is not fussy about conditions, growing happily in sun or part shade. Average moisture is adequate, but a little more or less works fine too.

Grasses in Shady Situations

Grasses and shade are compatible companions, although selecting grasses for shade requires a bit more investigation than for sunny sites. Deep shade is too challenging for most grasses; however, dappled or partial shade works for quite a few. How much shade is too much? Becoming familiar with your landscape will help you identify areas that receive more or less sun. Talk to experts, check books out of the library, and finally, as I have done in many instances, take a chance and experiment. If a plant does not look healthy, remember that it can always be moved, once, twice, or more, until it has a happy home. I recall a horticultural instructor I had years ago laughing as he told us he once moved a plant so many times it finally threw in the towel and died!

Between large and small rocks, the mopey bronze leafage of *Carex comans* (New Zealand hairy sedge) meanders through *Picea pungens* 'Glauca Procumbens' (trailing blue spruce).

One plant that I hope I never lose is black mondo grass. The common name alone is enough to evoke curiosity. Its Latin name is *Ophiopogon planiscapus* 'Nigrescens', and botanically it isn't a grass at all but a member of the lily family. It's a slow clump-former, and once it matures it will likely remain under a foot high. Black mondo grass is noted for its arresting foliage that begins as deep green at the bottom. As the season progresses, the color gradually changes from green to a very dark purple that is almost asphalt-black, from the bottom to the top of the plant. Toward the top, the narrow leaves flare open gradually. To the touch, the leaves feel starchy yet smooth. The small flower tips look like diluted red wine that has stained a white linen tablecloth. In my morning-sun area, these blooms begin in midsummer and last for a few weeks. I'm overjoyed to have this alluring plant and grateful to the friend who passed it on to me. Although it appears durable, I suspect that in a bad winter, say zero to lower, I will lose it unless I mulch it heavily.

When my mondo grass fills in more, it will curl up to the white flowers of *Lamium maculatum* 'White Nancy,' which is nestled nearby. Another good companion for it, although I have not grown these plants together, would be *Lamium galeobdolon* 'Herman's Pride' (yellow archangel). Years ago I used this perennial and was impressed with its wide-sweeping display near a pine tree and a stark white wall. It has yellow flowers and variegated green-and-silver-speckled foliage, which would be out of this world next to the mondo grass. Be patient, since this groundcover takes a few years to spread. Be sure you specifically use the cultivar 'Herman's Pride' because the straight species, *L. galeobdolon*, spreads alarmingly. Yellow archangel works well in dry, shady sites too.

Currently encircling my mondo grass is *Corydalis ochroleuca*. This lacy groundcover, with its creamy hue, is an ideal candidate when paired up with the grass, spotlighting extreme variance between dark and light. Early in spring, before these two perennials begin their show, I had an intuitive flash to bring in blue flowers with these plants. I chose *Brunnera macrophylla* (heartleaf Brunnera), which has dainty blue forget-me-not flowers. The large heart-shaped leaves increase in size once the flowers have faded. Combined with the other plants in this scene, this large-foliaged plant exemplifies the theme of contrast: dark against light, big opposed to small. There are a few cultivars of mondo grass. Two others are *O. planiscapus* 'Ebony Knight' and *O. japonicus* 'Kyoto'. Both are dark-colored low creepers that like moist soil.

A low groundcover grass that is a pleasure to admire when I head out my front door in spring and summer is *Holcus mollis* 'Variegatus' (creeping soft grass). I like to stroke its bright white-and-green-striped leaves; they feel soft and smooth, so the common name fits it to a T. The tactile nature of the greenery is of great value in gardens designed for people with visual handicaps. Some gardeners have found that this grass moves quickly through

The feathery tops of *Helictotrichon sempervirens* (blue avena or blue oat grass) float above
the red flowers of *Knautia macedonica* and barely touch the pink daisy *Senicio polydon rhodes.*
Photograph by Robert Bridges.

small sunny spaces. Mine is planted in partial shade and does not receive excessive moisture, so it has not been a rampant spreader. This grass too would be an excellent companion to black mondo grass, creating an original duo. The dark contrasts with light, but the plants have similar shapes, which makes a zesty pair. This form rarely flowers. A similar species, *Holcus lanatus*, has lovely white flowers tinted purple and reaches three feet tall. Commonly known as velvet grass because its foliage is so soft to touch, it self-sows readily and has naturalized in North America and other parts of the world.

If you have the space and choose to give more moisture to your *Holcus mollis* 'Variegatus', I suggest planting a hosta nearby. I have one token hosta, *Hosta sieboldiana* 'Frances Williams'. Some years it performs adequately, but often it requires more water than I choose to give it, so it sulks. On the East or West Coast, where moisture is more plentiful, these plants look full and lush and often reach three or four feet in height. This form, with its big, blue-green leaves touched with golden edges, is a popular plant at garden centers. The crinkled leaves are almost five inches across, and the plant has white flowers in summer. I rarely recommend growing two plants with variegated foliage next to each other because the area would look like a circus, but this is an exception. These two plants work well together, since the bold roundish leaves of the hosta, which is a bit taller, contrast with the linear lines of the creeping soft grass.

A woodland grass that towers above these last two plants is *Hystrix patula* (bottlebrush grass). Native to the eastern United States, it is an attractive flowering accent that definitely would zip up any lightly shaded border. Every time I see it blooming in summer I am tempted to purchase more of it because of its unusual showy beige panicles. Grouping a half dozen together would exhilarate the visual sense. The common name is clearly descriptive of this plant, with its bristly flowerheads that resemble bottlebrushes. It is a clump-forming grass that grows to almost three feet. It prefers a little extra moisture, but can tolerate a wide range of conditions, including dry shade. It does resent hot, dry conditions in full sun. I particularly like it because it gives this area an informal appearance, especially when I complete the picture and scatter digitalis (foxglove) and aconitum (monkshood) here and there.

Another grasslike plant that adds an informal splash to this garden is *Luzula sylvatica* (greater woodrush). A story comes with this grass relative, as it does with many special plants in my garden. On a rose tour years ago I met Graham Stuart Thomas and briefly chatted with him. His books are great as references and guides for new and experienced gardeners alike. One I use often when I teach is *The Rock Garden and Its Plants*. In it he mentions greater woodrush, saying some people won't give it garden room, but he feels it has many redeeming features, such as its ability to cover difficult sites and the fact that it is ideal between prickly shrubs. A year or so later, as I was browsing a specialized nursery, I saw it on the shelf and bought it instantly. In addition to what Graham Stuart Thomas says, I like its straplike, thick green leaves, which reach a foot high in my garden. The leaves are accented with occasional fine curly hairs along the margins. The small yellow-green panicles emerge in spring on thin stalks, reaching another ten inches. These flowers are not tremendously appealing on their own, but I do like it when the tiny bell-like seedheads mature and turn chestnut brown in fall.

Aside from doing the research when I put grasses in my shade garden, I try to go for as much diversity as I see fit; texture and lines are extremely critical. But I have confidence in my inner sense of design. I like variety here, but I do not want to end up with too many lines, because flowers are as essential to the overall scheme as the straight lines in this shade garden.

My Carex Phase

Carexes (sedges) are one of my current plant fascinations. I saw them awhile back and was intrigued by their shapes and long leaves. The word "carex" comes from the Greek *keiro*, meaning "to cut," alluding to the leaf margins, which are often sharp. Personally, although I have grown only a dozen or so, I have not found them to be too sharp, just curious to look at. There are over two thousand species of these grasslike perennial herbs! Some are suited to home gardens because of their ornamental value, while others need to be relegated to wilder or milder climates or not brought into the home garden at all because of their aggressive nature. There are many compact varieties great for the small garden. They rival true grasses for their beauty in color and form. In shades of blue, yellow, and various greens and browns, they make unique specimens, groundcovers, and accents in the garden. Some, such as *Carex pendula* (weeping sedge), have interesting seed spikes and would be good choices for fresh and dried arrangements. Carexes are normally associated with damp woodland shady sites, but many are adaptable to sun with adequate moisture.

Among my favorites are *C. comans* (New Zealand hairy sedge) and *C. buchananii* (leatherleaf sedge). I have been growing the first one for many years. It is located at the bottom of one of my rock gardens, which helps it receive adequate moisture. To many gardeners, some carexes are just plain brown, ugly, and dead looking. As I like to say, in psychological lingo, I have a positive transference to them, meaning that I am attracted to them and like their appearance. *C. comans* has a moppy dome shape and is bronze to tawny brown. The fine-textured leaves reach about eighteen inches, but back East or in the

Northwest this foliage may eventually grow to six feet! In the Rocky Mountain West they stay low to the ground, opening up in the middle and spreading their foliage all around. Their petite grainlike flowers have some ornamental value, appearing in fall along the tips of the stems as they lie on the ground. This past spring is the first time I have sheared the foliage down to three or four inches. I know this will encourage new growth and probably

CARE OF GRASSES

Soil Needs

My approach to soil preparation with all of my grasses is very simplified and random. I *never* do anything special for the site. I do basic amending in almost all of my flower beds because many perennials need organic matter in some form. I'm careful not to make the soils too rich or extremely lean, although most grasses are tolerant of poor soils and in fact perform quite admirably in whatever you have prepared. I try to create a balance between these two poles, but I rarely think about the process for more than two minutes!

Planting and Spacing

This part of the process is quite intuitive and easy too. Dig the hole and plant. Generally, I plant the grass at the same level at which it was growing in the pot, pressing it securely around the edges to make sure it bonds with the soil. Then I nurture it with water and try not to forget a week later where I planted it! Sometimes I've studied the plant or seen it in public or private gardens, so I have an idea about its needs. Other times, it's all guesswork. Again, I figure all plants can be moved, if either the plant or the gardener is unhappy with the location.

I also trust my intuition as to how far apart to plant grasses. Sometimes I'll use one specimen; other times I may want to group a few depending upon what feels right for the site. There is really no right or wrong approach, although I once saw an expert plant two specimens of *Miscanthus sinensis* 'Gracillimus' within a foot of each other. I personally think it was the designer's lack of knowledge rather than a desire for a massing effect. This grass should be planted four or five feet apart so that its full beauty and drama can be seen. Planting clumps too close also inhibits growth potential. A good rule of thumb for most grasses is to place them as far apart as their eventual height. A few things to consider: How fast do you want them to cover the area? What is your budget? What is your aesthetic goal? Often new gardeners err on the side of planting grasses too closely; sometimes it's hard to imagine how large they'll become when you bring them home in average-size nursery containers. It's particularly important not to plant the larger ones too close to walkways and driveways.

bring in more coppery fresh tones. When I completed this simple task, I chuckled a bit, because my memory flashed on the clean-looking crewcuts teenage boys and men received when they went to the barbershop in the 1950s and 1960s.

Originally I planted just one of these sedges, but it has happily spread over the years, creating a mass planting, which pleases me. If too many show up, it is not too much trouble

---

Dividing Ornamental Grasses

Most of these plants are undemanding, but it is still necessary to notice what is happening to them. Each plant is different, and some need more frequent division than others. Watch for telltale signs. Is the grass dying out in the center? Is it not flowering as well as it has in the past? Have the trees in the area gotten too large so that now this sun lover finds itself in too shady a spot? Has it been ten years since it was first planted? If so, perhaps it's time to rip out the entire plant and start over. Sometimes, over years, weeds have crept into the center of the plant and digging the plant up would make it easier to remove them. Or it might be time to trash the entire grass and buy a new one!

For the majority of grasses, in late winter or early spring, cut the foliage back to make it easier to do the dividing. Cut them back at this time even if they do not need division. This is a ritual for most grasses. Use pruners or loppers depending on the size of the grass; for some of the giant ones, you might need a strong saw or even a chain saw. In most cases you need to be ruthless, cutting these large grasses down to a few inches. I prune grasses to about four to eight inches. Remember, this does not harm them; it stimulates them to begin their new growth cycle. With *Helictotrichon sempervirens* (blue avena grass or blue oat grass), I usually leave about eight inches on the plant, which otherwise might take too long to recover, although I secretly suspect that if you should accidentally shear it way back one year, it too would eventually come back. Use grass clippings as mulch in your garden, or recycle in whatever way you feel would be best for you and the environment.

The next step is to dig the whole clump out of the ground. Keep the clump intact and get as much of the root system out as possible. If the clump is large, work gradually yet deeply around its edges. Once the clump is out, carry it to an open area where it will be accessible. Use a sharp spade to divide it into as many pieces as you desire, depending on how mature the grass is. When I divide my grasses I use a sharp edging tool that works wonders. Wearing strong-soled shoes, I place the tool in the plant and jump on it a few times. On occasion I have ruined a few stems with this approach; however, grasses are resilient and generally remain unscathed by my harsh treatment. I'll remove any weak stems and try to get the best-looking and healthiest pieces to replant, and the cycle begins. After certain grasses have been in for six or seven years, as was the case with *M. sinensis* 'Yaku Jima', I'll dig up my three plants, and divide them; then I'll plant some in my garden and give others away to friends. (If grasses are too large to lift alone, I suggest getting assistance.) And so it goes. ∎

to weed them out. Down the road, if it does become a nuisance, I will weed it out entirely. This carex tumbles among my black and red granite rocks and spills over my stony path. A few feet up from here and jutting over my rocks is *Picea pungens* 'Glauca Procumbens' (trailing blue spruce). This spruce has pencil-point-sharp blue needles. The carex might look brown, dead, and dull on its own, but next to the rocks and the blue spruce, it becomes a substantial feature.

I've been growing *Carex buchananii* for a number of years. Since it is native to New Zealand, I feel fortunate to have had it as long as I have. I suspect that I might lose it if we didn't get adequate snow cover, or if the temperatures fell to minus ten degrees F. or colder. Its uncommon coppery red and brown color makes it a desirable accent plant. It stands tall, growing almost two feet high. The vertical skinny foliage does not bend much, unlike that of some other carexes, which helps make it a team player. Any daisy with a center-raised disk would be a superb companion plant. I have used *Rudbeckia fulgida* var. *sullivantii* 'Goldsturm' (black-eyed Susan) and *Echinacea purpurea* (purple coneflower); fall and winter change the coloration of these daisies to shades of brown and black, offering a breathtaking scene of browns, blacks, and the coppery tones of *C. buchananii*.

Another carex, native to the mountains of Japan, is *C. morrowii* 'Variegata' (Japanese sedge). This plant is a superb selection for a small shady garden. In an eye-catching scene, I have seen about eight of these ten-inch-high evergreen plants grouped closely together, their white-and-green-striped leaves and open habit bringing a flare of brightness to a dark corner. These long-lived plants are tolerant of a wide range of soils. From my experience, adding compost to the soil would be beneficial to their overall performance in a shady situation. In fall and part of winter they look attractive when almost fused with the paddle-shaped, thick, leathery, rusty maroon leaves of *Bergenia cordifolia* (heartleaf).

A carex that I have more as an oddity than as a very attractive plant is *C. muskingumensis* (palm sedge). The foliage resembles palm fronds, and it forms long arching clumps. Mostly a shade plant, it has worked for me in sun with ample moisture. I've noticed over the years that even though I do not water excessively, this and many other plants do well for me because of the siting of my backyard garden. Near a major street, my plot is many feet below the street level, and it gets more than sufficient runoff when we have spring rains. This carex, like many of mine, I plant near my paths so that garden visitors can observe the distinctive leaf structure as they stroll by. This sedge is not known for its showy flowers, so I suggest surrounding it with such plants as *Sisyrinchium angustifolium* (blue-eyed grass), a low-growing, irislike perennial that blooms for a long while, as well as the taller *Iris pseudacorus* (yellow flag iris). Both will tolerate moister soils, but are also adaptable when soils are a bit dryer too.

Because they are not true grasses, most carexes do not have the showy panicles that Mother Nature (with occasional help from breeders and propagators) has artistically arranged at the tops of a great number of grasses. The shapes and structures of carexes are simpler than those found in the larger, more complex family of grasses, which boasts over nine thousand species! Metaphorically speaking, they are good friends with grasses, but are not directly related, because they are in different plant families. Whether we choose true grasses or grasslike plants, gardeners are offered almost unlimited varieties to bring punch to any style of garden.

Wheat-colored sprays of *Pennisetum alopecroides* (fountain grass)
topple above the yellow-tinged leaves of *Amsonia tabernaemontana* (blue star).

CHAPTER SIX

The Richness of Color and Form

Fall Colors and Textures

As fall approaches, nudging both the landscape and the gardener, we may still have spurts of toasty weather, but thankfully the sunny hot days of summer shrink into the background. Intense heat and sunshine fade. This thrills me. After spending more than a decade working as a landscape contractor, I have grown weary of the sun's rays beating down on me, and the coming of fall is always quite a relief. During my landscaping years, I would dine at local eateries on weekends; while

Above: The red leaves of *Prunos besseyi* (western sand cherry) look attractive next to the chartreuse blooms of *Chrysothamnus nauseosus* (rabbitbrush).

145

most folks flocked to the bright and sunny patios, I would beg hostesses to seat me in a shady nook or inside where the air conditioning blasted so strongly that I might need a sweater. On a workday, if the weather turned out to be cloudy or overcast, I would cheer!

But fall is also the season for natural adjustments in color harmony. Frequent changes occur during spring and summer too, but fall and winter are indeed triumphant, offering every bit as much pleasure to the senses as does the other half of the gardening year. Drying plants and late bloomers gradually transform in the garden. An artistic fall and winter garden can be an utterly beautiful spectacle, composed of dramatic structures, evergreen plants, exotic seedheads, graceful grasses, and shades of red galore. For me, autumn in the garden is heaven, although it can be hectic, what with bulb planting, a minimal amount of cleanup, and bed preparation for the following spring. But it is definitely a serene and glorious season, and these cool, crisp months can be genuinely quite festive.

Autumn is the season of flame and bright gold, but my landscape also presents silver, deep purple, beige, and orange tones. As I stroll my gravelly paths and grassy areas, I admire various shrubs and perennials. For instance, for a number of years I have been growing *Aronia melanocarpa* (black chokeberry). I consider this low-growing shrub an especially worthwhile addition during these cooler months as it turns brilliant red. The black, crinkly fruits that appeared in summer remain on the plant through much of the winter, attracting birds and providing still more color.

Over time it will sucker, but after six years, that has not been a problem in my garden because I keep the soil lean and skimp on additional water. And, if the shrub does begin to sucker, I'll just cut the stems to the ground, thus restricting its spread.

Next to the chokeberry, I randomly placed an easy-care perennial and a grass. *Amsonia tabernaemontana* (blue star) has starry blue flowers in spring, but, as temperatures cool, the glossy leaves along stiff stems become yellow, harmonizing with the red Aronia. Completing the triad is the tawny grass *Pennisetum alopecuroides* (fountain grass), which generally grows three feet high and as wide. The inflorescences of this clump-forming grass resemble large foxtails. It is versatile, dependable, and, in my opinion, one of the showiest of all the ornamental grasses. After a number of years (about six in my region), it will "seed around." In other words, seedlings appear in other sections of the garden as well as, usually, closer to the original clump. Again, I key into my intuition, which tells me whether I am pleased with where it has spontaneously surfaced. If I like where it has popped up I'll leave it, while other times I'll demote it to the compost heap. Sometimes for fun in late fall, I might encircle the old flowers midway with my fingers and gently pull up on the soft seedheads, scattering the fuzzy particles and leaving behind narrow, naked stems. I imagine that children walking in wild fields or meadows would giggle and have fun with this activity.

Along a narrow strip I have brought together more shrubs and perennials whose strength is fall foliage. They demonstrate that dry gardens, when designed creatively, can be outstanding. *Seriphidium canum* (silver sagebrush) is planted near my mailbox, where it receives no water other than rainfall. *Chrysothamnus nauseosus* (rabbitbrush) and *Prunus besseyi* (Western sand cherry) are its companions there.

I have grown rabbitbrush for ten years next to my driveway, where its wild, unkempt habit constantly annoyed me by blocking access to my truck. Finally, I decided to go radical. (At this stage it was about five feet high and five feet wide.) One day in late winter I hesitantly (fearing that I might damage or lose it forever) sheared this shrub down to eight inches. Now it looked pretty pathetic, but I kept my fingers crossed. In early spring new shoots emerged from the gnarly, woody stems, and I cheered with joy! When fall came around, the yellow flowers, gray foliage, and pale yellow and green stems were more vibrant than ever. This solved my car door problem and gave the shrub a refreshed and tidy look. I'm sure I'll need to repeat this radical cutback every few years. Because *Seriphidium canum* has been growing there just as long, seemingly ruthless pruning techniques will stimulate it to put out new growth as well.

The normal height of *Prunus besseyi* is four or five feet. However, my particular specimen is a foot shorter and somewhat contorted. Some of this may be due to its dry site, but I also think it is just oddly formed. This plant usually has a rather round habit, but mine is shaped like a recumbent egg, with branches that bend downwards, hugging a nearby rock. Many white flowers appear on it in spring, and it makes a particularly splendid companion to the rabbitbrush and the pewter-toned sage in late fall, when it flaunts spiffy red leaves.

P. besseyi is not fussy about soil conditions: Clay or a sandy loam will do fine. A great foundation and xeriscape plant, it grows natively in the grasslands of eastern Colorado, even up to eight thousand feet in elevation, and through western and central Kansas.

For added punch, I have planted *Perovskia atriplicifolia* (Russian sage) here for its long spikes of lavender-blue flowers. These four unique and individual elements melt into one very harmonious fall vignette.

Another prime shrub in autumn, one that also gives structure to my rock garden, is *Cotoneaster apiculatus* 'Tom Thumb' (cranberry cotoneaster). This twiggy creeper, which remains low, makes a bold fall statement when its small green leaves change to fire-engine red. Around the shrub I have placed plants with other structures and colors, all of which magnify the red of 'Tom Thumb'. *Festuca glauca* (blue fescue) and *Chamaebatiaria millefolium* (fernbush), noted for its lacy gray and often evergreen leaves, both grow there. The fernbush nuzzles up to a granite boulder streaked with red and black so that, even if the leaves fall off, its curving stems create an impressive coarse silhouette for winter.

The greenery of *Miscanthus sinensis* 'Yaku Jima' twists comfortably through the flowers
and stems of rose 'Ferdy'. Front and center, *Geranium sanguinum* (bloody cranesbill)
hugs the pea gravel alongside the marble-sized flowers of *Scabiosa columnifera* (pincushion flower).

When fall is still at its peak, other plants, like magnets, vie for my attention. Except in the dead of winter and early in spring, when they just begin to emerge, the hardy geraniums (commonly known as cranesbills) are beloved flowers of mine. Their crocheted-looking foliage is superb. I enjoy *Geranium sanguineum* (bloody cranesbill), a plant familiar to avid gardeners, which acts as a carpet beneath the Meidiland rose 'Ferdy'™ put in the right spot (more about these roses later in this chapter). For weeks in early summer this low, cushiony geranium produces scores of deep pink flowers, and in fall the leaves are abundant with good autumn tints. Surprisingly, it grows well even in fairly dry conditions. A gardening friend of mine who lived nearby grew it for years in an unirrigated spot, this plant being satisfied with the low rainfall the Denver area receives. Now, seven years after she sold her house, this plant continues to bloom, in spite of the fact that the new owners are non-gardeners, and the geranium, along with the rest of the garden, is neglected.

Two other cranesbills that bring zest to the fall garden are *G. macrorrhizum* (big-root geranium) and *G. himalayense* 'Plenum' (syn. *G. himalayense* 'Birch Double'). The deeply cut foliage of *G. macrorrhizum* forms thick mats in sun or light shade, and in both situations the leaves turn potent autumn tints. Moreover, the foliage is aromatic when gently rubbed.

G. himalayense 'Plenum' is a delight to grow; it has puffy, double, blue-violet flowers, the size of quarters, on small plants. As Thanksgiving approaches, I notice that its wavy foliage is polished with autumn color.

Seasonal Changes with Seedpods and Foliage

After the holiday commotion of Christmas and New Year's has fizzled down, and sometimes even before it cranks up, I take time to move slowly through my garden. Besides admiring the glimmering shades of autumn, I pay particular attention to significant forms and textures. There is such variety in plant structure evident at this time of year, and many

As fall sneaks up on the garden, the fading flowers of *Verbena bonariensis* appear to dance in front of the fluffy plumage of *Miscanthus sinensis* 'Yaku Jima'.

plants charm me with their unparalleled characteristics. In my front, partially shaded garden, I grow the perennial *Baptisia australis* (false indigo), whose flowers of a soft blue appear in spring. Then, in fall, I delight to see its thick, two-inch-long seedpods turn black-purple. This color tells me that when I cut the stems down, I will be able to shake them and hear the rattling sound of the many brown seeds within. Often visitors to my garden are curious about these odd, puffy-looking, dark-colored seedpods, so I'll clip some and watch facial expressions as they jiggle the stems like rattles. At this stage in the life of the plant, stems and pods make an excellent addition to any dried bouquet.

Some of the most peculiar, yet elegant, seedpods are those of the trailing groundcover *Oenothera macrocarpa* (Missouri evening primose). A good plant choice for a dry and sunny location, it blooms sunshine yellow in cooler evening hours. In fall and winter its large, papery thin, golden fruit pods add unusual complexity, so I often leave them on the plant late into spring. (If I were a propagator, I could easily obtain the seeds for this plant simply by tipping the foursquare capsule and pouring the morsels into the palm of my hand; they germinate easily.) In their winter dress, they are also festive in a holiday centerpiece.

To complement the seedpods of the oenothera, try any low, evergreen form of veronica, such as *V. liwanensis* (Turkish speedwell), which is smothered with iridescent blue flowers in spring, or the hairy-leaved *V. pectinata* (woolly veronica), which also has blue flowers. Two superb veronicas for late-season interest are the silver-leafed *V. cinerea* and, a new one to my garden, *V.* 'Waterperry Blue'. The latter is a superior choice that has red-stained, round, serrated leaves. I have planted this crawler along my flagstone path, where it forms clusters of foliage that drape over the red stones. Because the path curves and slopes to a small degree, I imagine this combination as a "river of red."

Another specimen, unsurpassed for its unusual form, is *Acanthus hungaricus*—(bear's breeches). This flower can be a little finicky for some gardeners because it prefers exactly the right conditions in order to give a royal show. All species of acanthus require good drainage and are especially averse to wet winters, so gardeners need to pay strict attention to where water or snow collects at particular sites and avoid those spots. My plant grows a few feet high in full sun, although I know that it would bloom better in partial shade and that shading it from the intense afternoon sunlight would prevent its leaves from sometimes scorching. In winter, the top six inches holds oblique, pearly particles and brown seed capsules topped off with spines. It is a strangely shaped plant, looking like many candelabras massed together. It would fit very well surrounding a castle in the Middle Ages, especially with its summer-blooming spikes of white and purple flowers. It definitely deserves to be planted more widely.

Also deserving of more recognition are the *Euphorbia*s (spurges). I discussed euphorbias in Chapter Two, but one I consider noteworthy in fall and early winter is *E. seguieriana*.

The species name commemorates the French botanist J. F. Séguier (1704–1784), who described the flora of Verona, Italy, at a time when his countrymen were involved in a series of wars to dominate the Continent. In my region this graceful plant grows over a foot high and as wide, with tiny gray-and-blue leaves in spring; compressed along the stems, the leaves give a bushy effect. By June they have turned lime-yellow, a color that continues through summer, and then the foliage shifts into rainbow shades of reds, purples, and green, becoming more intense as fall chugs along. As frost lingers on the plant and the stems languish, it retains its vivid colors and becomes a plant to appreciate during chilly weather.

In the wild, this species is found in a variety of dry habitats. I tried to imitate those conditions and planted it in a partially dry section of my garden where the gravelly soil drains well. With extra water, the center of the plant will be open and floppy, although still attractive. Whichever way you choose to grow this euphorbia, frame it with plants that heighten its charm. Use any form of *Festuca* (fescue), with narrow blue foliage that flatters the texture and colors of the euphorbia. For height, add *Perovskia atriplicifolia* (Russian sage). I like repeating similar plants in different spots throughout my garden; it helps knit the elements nicely together.

A rose species unfamiliar to most gardeners, but one I feel honored to have, is *Rosa hemisphaerica*. I came across it rather serendipitously a number of years ago. During an unusually calm moment in spring—if there ever is such a thing—I was savoring the floral display at the Denver Botanic Gardens Rock Alpine Garden. I also noticed many small potted plants stacked along a shaded fence, awaiting their special planting time. Panayoti was out and about tending to his dear children the plants, but, as often happens, he had to give me a tour to show me some wonderful blooming flowers that I would admire, gush over, and wish I had in my garden! At the end of our visit, as we headed toward the shaded fence area, Panayoti bent over and handed me a small plant, saying, "Try this rose. A friend who grew it from seed gave it to me, and I'll never get around to planting it!" I quickly grabbed it, ecstatic to explore something new, particularly a rose. At that time I was beginning my love affair with shrub roses.

I walked around with it for a few minutes at home until I saw a good spot. It was barely a four-inch stick at this stage of its life; I planted it at the bottom of a berm and gave it a lot of tender loving care. Then I researched the rose and discovered it to be a rare find. (In my intuitive fashion, I tend to do things topsy-turvy; I put the plant in the ground, then I learn about it.) Rosarian Graham Stuart Thomas believes *Rosa hemisphaerica*, which is the double form, was grown before 1625, and is from Western Asia. The single form, which I have, is a native of Asiatic Turkey to northwestern Iran, and, according to some authorities, might be *R. hemisphaerica rapinii*. (In the complex world of rose experts, confusion sometimes surrounds origins of these very antique roses. For those readers seeking the very latest authoritative research, I recommend *The Old Rose Adventurer* by Brent Dickerson.) The double form of this rose usually does not have perfect blooms in wet climates, where it tends to "ball" and decay without opening; it prefers warm, dry weather. The single, slightly cupped form doesn't flower profusely either, but that is irrelevant to me; I'm pleased to have such an ancient specimen in my garden. It captivates me to realize that this rose was happily growing in Turkey and Iran while other nations were doing battle to devastate the Holy Roman Empire during the complex Thirty Years' War, from 1618 to 1648, and that in

Texture and form come alive by the cat and the stone, as the tall fan-shaped Miscanthus sp. grass dominates the scene. The Aster provides touches of purple, complemented by sprigs of *Genista lindheimeri* (broom).

Although color is mostly absent here, the feel of fabric (plants) is brought to life by the complex-patterned daisy flower *Eryginum planum* (sea holly), as well as the plumose flowerheads of *Calamagrostis brachytricha* (Korean feather reed grass).

the same period the English Puritans known as Pilgrims were establishing American colonies at Plymouth Rock to escape religious persecution in England!

In fall, the tiny orange-and-yellow leaves of *R. hemisphaerica rapinii* glimmer in the midday sun, and there is some sporadic rebloom. In winter I treasure its upstanding, prickly red stems that fan outwards. To complement the fall foliage, I grow *Tanacetum densum* subsp. *amani* (partridge feather) at its base, where the low-growing silver foliage spreads in a half circle like a big smile.

What to Do in the Dead of Winter

In winter, unless passionate gardeners are ordering plants through the plethora of catalogs that begin to arrive in their mailboxes—and now through their computers—in January, many get a bit "itchy." Even *while* ordering plants, many are restless. The question is, "What to do?" The ground is frozen in most spots. Of course, pruning is possible when weather allows. Bundling up is easy and time is available; there isn't an urgency to attend to other garden chores. I move at a snail's pace. In some years, to no avail, I have tried futilely to hack at the frozen yet weedy ground; sparks fly when the metal tool hits the solid crystallized soil!

During the winter season, if you are a seed fanatic, or have a greenhouse, or enjoy stratifying seed, your energy can be channeled to these avenues. Playing with your garden's design is another popular choice. Or maybe you'll take a class from a landscape design expert. To see what ideas stimulate your intuition and imagination as you dream about the coming seasons, you may check out books from the local library or your nearest botanic garden. In your cozy, warm house you could roughly draw designs; if you're not pleased with your plant choices, it is quite simple to erase them or scribble them out and experiment again. Let your imagination go wild and see what ideas spontaneously click with your intuition.

Another option is to take a vacation to a warm sunny spot. I know of gardeners who relish this prospect. Many people, if they can't actually get away, attend garden events at local botanic gardens where, in large auditoriums, they salivate over plant introductions and beautiful flowers presented by world-famous gardeners and local experts who travel about giving slide shows. Gardeners go "ooh" and "ah" and, squinting in dimly lit halls, quickly jot down notes about plants that they have fallen in love with and must have. At these events there is "bonding" among, and between, novice and well-seasoned gardeners. They visit, laugh, and share past and present garden experiences while catching up on family affairs and local gossip.

In winter, I might teach a class on one of many garden subjects or prepare a slide presentation for a local garden center. I also like to write about gardening, so I'll roll up my sleeves, let the juices flow, and dream up an article as I sit at my computer and gaze out at my snow-covered landscape.

A task that arose for me this past January was that of dealing with the seven cubic yards of well-composted manure and fill dirt sitting in my driveway. I had it delivered when the weather was mild; then, suddenly, temperatures dipped to ten degrees and six inches of snow piled up fast. I had to be patient, but gradually I moved it to my backyard. I always hope I'll be lucky enough to find a younger person to help me. In years past I was able to pack my wheelbarrow with this luscious material, but this year, when I turned fifty-four, I was aware that I carry less soil in the wheelbarrow and that my pace has slowed.

Fall and winter come to our lives as well as to our gardens. Gardening is a suitable activity for people of any age, although adjustments need to be made as our bodies mature and age limits our physical abilities. Some gardeners accept the fact that they finally need helpers. Others move to smaller sites, and still others have small gardens off their patios or balconies. Raised beds are another option that suits many gardeners. With this method we sit or kneel on chairs (some fitted with wheels) as we maneuver around the garden. Special garden tools are widely available to assist older gardeners who have developed crippling arthritis or other maladies that affect the limbs. Check your local garden center or botanic garden for more information on this topic.

Winter Structure and Leaves

Winter's downtime lets me survey leafless trees and shrubs as they stand out in the garden, backed by crisp blue-and-white skies. They offer pleasing branching habits and are attractive with their individual patterns of growth. Although aspens are not my favorite tree in the West (because they perform better at elevations above six thousand feet), their vertical lines and their stark white bark flecked with dark grooves are eye-catching in the winter landscape. My eyes are also drawn to crabapple trees, with their huddle of branches and lingering colorful fruits. Branches and trunks of many other trees are vivid with dimpled textures and exhibit restful colors like deep burgundy and shades of walnut, green, and gray.

Some deciduous shrubs and small trees, such as viburnums, hold onto their leaves late into winter and beyond. They appear to paint the sky with masterly floral-colored foliage. They are especially agreeable, as are other deciduous specimens, when planted among the conical or broad shapes of statuesque evergreens. The fruits of viburnums are shades of blue/black, purple, orange, and red, adding enormous appeal as they age and dry through the winter. I heartily agree with Dr. Michael Dirr, professor of horticulture at the University of Georgia and author of *Manual of Woody Landscape Plants*, when he states, "A garden without a viburnum is akin to life without music and art."

With or without surrounding evergreen trees, viburnums are exceptional choices for the devoted gardener. Two of my favorites are *Viburnum carlesii* (Korean spice viburnum) and *V. lentago* (nannyberry). I have grown the former for ten years, and I love the intense fragrance it emits in spring from blush-pink buds that open to mounds of white flowers. A popular choice for homeowners and landscape designers alike, it surrounds the rose garden at the White House. I've pruned my specimen of this shrub only once in its lifetime to allow more light and air into its center.

V. lentago has a tall, thin form, with white, flat-headed flowers. Its winter gear includes black fruit and long, pointed leaves ablaze with red color. I have found it to be a very slow grower, ultimately reaching ten to fifteen feet. This appeals to me since it does not overwhelm my landscape, yet it is versatile for the back of a perennial border or as an accent near a bench or in a quiet corner. Mildew, its common ailment in moister climates, does not affect this viburnum in my region. To deter mildew problems, plant where air circulation is excellent.

An agreeable small shrub that gives a boon to the winter landscape is *Rhus aromatica* 'Gro-Low' (fragrant sumac). This wide-spreading shrub, useful for erosion control and covering difficult sites, has small yellow flowers in spring. In winter its short woody stems

Despite some rules about planting ornamental grasses a certain distance from other plants, I tossed these rules to the wind when I planted the tall, billowing *Miscanthus sinenis* 'Variegatus' virtually smack up against *Eupatorium maculatum* 'Gateway' (Joe pye weed).

The delicate crestlike features of *Calamagrostis acutiflora* 'Overdam' (variegated feather reed grass) enliven and bring movement to this combination, as the buttery yellow flowers of rose 'Golden Wings' shine in the background.

crisscross through the maroon branches of a tall species shrub rose, *Rosa eglanteria* (sweetbriar). Emphasizing this combination is the top of the well-branched sumac, which appears speckled with dots of hairy red fruits. Both of these plants are particularly showy against my blue-painted house.

Early in winter, as I glance out at my landscape chilled by a dusting of recent snow, I am drawn to leaves of perennials and shrubs that resist falling to the ground. They are in no hurry to expose their naked stems and branches; many hang limp, with a shriveled appearance, as if saying, "Leave me alone, I'll drop in good time." As they gradually release themselves, and when temperatures rise a bit, I will take a few hours and clean up. I'll clip tacky-looking dead brown stems from the previous season, rake tattered leaves, and tend to other simple tasks. I enjoy this break from the intensity of the spring and summer garden. During these months my ideas become constellated as I explore them. I take more time to keenly observe foliage and flower mergers that titillate me, and think of where I may want to move certain plants once the ground defrosts and spring erupts. On a daily basis, I watch my garden carefully evolve as some perennial foliage withers and deteriorates early, while time and weather alter the apparel of other plants.

Standing Tall

Gardeners grow disheartened during winter as many plants are slowly crushed, succumbing to the white blanket of snow. However, in spite of the snow, the ornamental grasses often remain vertical. The rigors of fall and winter fail to diminish the elegance of many of them: In fact, to many gardeners, these are the seasons when grasses give their ultimate show-stopping performances. They dazzle the visual sense and are "pumped" with energy, offering visual linear appeal in addition to a wide spectrum of textural and color variations.

This time of year, my eyes continually shift from one spot to another as I see impressive grass scenarios. *Miscanthus sinensis* 'Gracillimus' (maiden grass) is a star performer in my garden. Its cultivar name 'Gracillimus' speaks to its graceful appearance. Late in summer its wide, five-foot-tall vase shape and slender green foliage appoint it queen of the garden. The grass radiates majesty as though it were sitting on a throne, proclaiming, "This garden is *my* domain and *I am in charge.*" I have placed maiden grass about five feet from a path so it can be touched and admired. In the fall, as I walk past it, I reach over and weave my fingers through the curved, narrow beige-and-orange-tinted leaves. As winter temperatures nip at the foliage, the leaf tips randomly curl, to further accentuate a whirlwind effect. There are many forms of miscanthus, all shimmering in their fall and winter effects. Their flower plumes are also great in dried arrangements, extending their appeal indoors. At this moment, on my office shelf, in a colorful flowerpot, I have a dried bouquet that has a few grasses in it, along with seedheads of dark-colored penstemons (beardtongue) and echinacea (coneflower), and the magenta stems and wrinkled, dark red hips of a shrub rose.

As I have toured gardens over the years, I have often seen grasses used innovatively. On one midautumn tour in private gardens in Pennsylvania, I saw *Miscanthus sinensis* 'Gracillimus' grouped in twenty separate bundles, which had been braided as though they were someone's long hair. The creative gardener had then twisted twine around each bundle from the bottom up, leaving the fluffy top inflorescence exposed. The result was an artistic green-and-tan spidery creation; or, more imaginatively, it looked like a monster from a horror movie invading the garden!

When I toured the J. C. Raulston Arboretum at North Carolina State University one winter, I saw a long, deep perennial border with many winter-dormant grasses standing straight against a bed of snow. For radical winter effect, a gardener had spray-painted on the sandy grasses, colorful horizontal stripes of orange, red, and blue throughout this border. It was a smash hit with garden visitors.

Ornamental grasses are extremely beautiful in their untouched state as well. Another miscanthus, smaller in stature than 'Gracillimus' and my absolute favorite grass, is *M. sinensis* 'Yaku Jima'. Passionate gardeners often have a favorite plant, which usually is whatever they are focused on at the moment. When I teach, I will swear that the plant I am showing at the moment is my absolute favorite; then I show another, saying, "No, this is my favorite," and so on. Laughter rolls from the audience as each new "favorite" pops up on the slide screen!

'Yaku Jima' was one of my early purchases years ago and has remained special for me. It was introduced to the United States in the mid-1970s by a plant-collecting expedition to Japan, sponsored by Longwood Gardens in Kennett Square, Pennsylvania. 'Yaku Jima' grows naturally on the island of Yakushima. Its habit is dense, and it begins its rise to stardom in summer, when it reaches about three feet in height and width and its foliage mimics the crinoline skirts of the 1950s. In autumn the leaves turn the color of toast, with traces of crimson. The grass remains attractive through winter as its flowery, off-white plumes go through numerous changes. In late summer, the inflorescences appear, which occupy the top six inches of the stems, and are softly pointed, much like gentle paintbrushes. Next they open full and woolly and are covered with hundreds of hairy spikelets that look like tiny crosses. Further along, as winter deepens its grip, the inflorescences become feathery. This grass, like many others, changes its appearance from one week to the next.

'Yaku Jima' is outstanding as a companion plant. In the midst of this grass and in front of it is the statuesque annual *Verbena bonariensis*. The species name bonariensis comes from the place where it was first discovered in 1726, Buenos Aires. Its small purple flowers are affected by seasonal changes; as the purple color dims, it turns rusty brown, still retaining hints of purple in the flower. Perched atop long stems, the blossoms assume the guise of polychromatic clouds that float in front of the miscanthus.

M. sinensis 'Variegatus' graces a prominent spot in my garden. It is one of the oldest cultivars of Japanese silver grass still available and has been grown in gardens since 1900. It continues to be popular, and I can definitely see why. The grass grows to about five feet in height, with cream-and-white-striped leaves that are three-quarters of an inch wide. The growth habit is slightly curved; it gradually droops more as the season progresses. The inflorescences are similar to those of 'Yaku Jima', but the stems are thicker. In late fall, as the foliage blanches to almond, the tips of the sturdy round stems are pointed and very sharp, reminiscent of bayonets used in armies from earlier times.

This specimen cradles close to *Eupatorium maculatum* 'Gateway' (Joe pye weed). Only one specimen of this plant is needed, as the stems shoot up five feet and are topped off by very large purple flowerheads that remind me of broccoli. Later, they turn shades of

Different colors and textures complement each other as Pumpkin gracefully strolls down the garden aisle.

burgundy with a fuzzy appearance. Long, pointed leaves and mahogany stems add substance to this combination, particularly when the green-and-white grassy foliage of the variegated miscanthus stretches into the eupatorium. I have massed a few plants of *Boltonia asteroides* 'Snowbank' as other companions in this area. The snowy flowers, with their delicate daisy faces on wiry gray-green stems, soften the vertical lines of the grass.

Another miscanthus to cheer about is *M. sinensis* var. *purpurascens* (flame grass). In my region, this plant grows from three to five feet tall, and it doesn't wait until fall to take center stage. The common name describes its bright red, late-summertime appearance well; later on, the foliage turns shades of maroon and holds that color well into winter. Even in light shade the leaves will be sensational in various pastel shades. If you have this grass in a lightly shaded area, try underplanting it with the round-leafed *Bergenia cordifolia* (heartleaf Bergenia). Dwarf pines are good choices too, as well as the often-evergreen foliage of *Euonymus fortunei* 'Coloratus' (purpleleaf winter creeper).

A final favorite grass, one that adds verticality next to an oval boulder, is *Miscanthus sinensis* 'Strictus' (porcupine grass). This narrow form holds its gold-banded leaves erect like porcupine quills, increasing the effectiveness of its variegation and amplifying its spiky

Photograph by Steve Silk, courtesy of *Fine Gardening* magazine

The pillowlike silver mound of *Artemisia pycnocephala* 'David's Choice' creates a dramatic scene when *Macleya cordata* (plume poppy) towers above it, while snapdragons add a spark of color.

effect. It flowers in midautumn with copper plumes. In the heart of winter the foliage has strong orange tones, with cream-colored, curving inflorescences standing atop round stems. This grass looks especially nice cloaked with a thin layer of snow.

The fun of using miscanthus grasses in the garden is only amplified when select perennials are grouped with them. As I've previously discussed, eupatoriums are excellent choices to combine among the taller varieties. Or try large daisy flowers such as heleniums (sneezeweed—honestly, not a weed at all, and it doesn't make you sneeze), or the easy-to-grow

Heliopsis helianthoides (false sunflower), loaded with brassy yellow blossoms. Shrub roses, with their wide spectrum of colors, globular shapes, and thorny stems, are stunning companions to ornamental grasses. Most Canadian or rugosa types will repeat-bloom in the fall. Low, ground-covering shrub roses can add luminescence to the base of any large grass. They will produce one strong flush of color in spring, and some will repeat-bloom in summer and fall. I personally favor the Meidiland shrub roses, which come from the firm of Meilland in France. 'Pink Meidiland'™ shows single, deep pink flowers with white centers and yellow stamens, while Ferdy'™ bears double coral-pink flowers on three-foot arching canes. In fall the leaves have a dark red sheen, and they resist falling until almost spring. A third Meidiland, which I have planted beneath *M. sinensis* 'Variegatus', is 'Sea Foam'™. It repeat-blooms with double white flowers in fall, and its rusty-red foliage also remains intact into winter.

When I shop for miscanthus varieties, I feel I am at a buffet and have a smorgasbord of flavors to casually choose from. In the year 2001, the mail-order catalog of Kurt Bluemel's well-stocked nursery in Baldwin, Maryland, listed more than sixty miscanthus cultivars. If you are a foliage fancier, I suggest you experiment with these grasses; I'm sure you'll find a few to fit your particular lifestyle and garden.

Emphatically living up to the phrase "standing tall" is *Saccharum ravennae*, formerly *Erianthus ravennae* (plume grass or hardy pampas grass). If *Miscanthus sinensis* 'Gracillimus' is the queen of my garden, *Saccharum ravennae* is most definitely the king. In fall, the stalks skyrocket to a height of at least ten feet and create a towering form in any garden. I highly recommend it to gardeners who can afford the space and want something majestic. Plant a few as a privacy screen or just one as a specimen.

In autumn, the foliage of *S. ravennae* turns beige, with tints of purple and orange. Toward the top, this grass is embellished with many flowering plumes, each of which is almost a foot long. I sometimes cut these plumes and bring them inside to spruce up my kitchen and living room. Because they are downy in texture, I can tie a few together so that they resemble a feather duster one might use for cobwebs that gather in ceiling corners and on light fixtures. However, I can't literally dust with these plumes because, when a sweeping motion is used against a hard surface, the dried particles begin to shatter, creating more work!

Recently, after six years, *S. ravennae* has begun to seed around in my garden, sprouting up unexpectedly in a few spots. In some places I'll leave it because I like its effect, especially when it serendipitously emerges at the bottom of a berm. To enhance its curling-skirt look, I have planted the low annual groundcover *Verbena* 'Imagination', with its round purple flowers.

Near my patio, where grasses can be seen up close and personal, I have laced a few in with shrub roses and perennials. The grasses add textural alternatives, as well as shades of wheat and almond to this "wild area." One grass that I have planted here is *Calamagrostis* x *acutiflora* 'Karl Foerster', whose tall, slender foliage blends easily among the colorful flowers. I placed it near the shrub rose 'New Face', a scene-stealer with its single, flat, wide-open blooms colored pink and white. The grass and the rose blend nicely with the many yellow flowers of fall that are planted there: *Ratibida columnifera* (Mexican hat), *Helenium* ssp. (sneezeweed), and *Rudbeckia triloba* (black-eyed Susan). Dangling wispily above a cluster of rudbeckias are a few fragile, pinky-white blossoms of *Gaura lindheimeri* 'Whirling Butterflies'. The flowers atop this four-foot plant bounce about with any gust of wind. It's a long bloomer and a definite plus for the summer/fall garden.

Also residing in this area is *Deschampsia caespitosa* var. *vivipara*, sometimes known as 'Fairy's Joke' (tufted hair grass). It is profuse with dense green tufts and tiny plantlets on thin, ethereal flower spikes. It's no joke that this grass can be aggressive if it's given too much moisture and rich soil, but I like its glitzy green color and uncommon plumes.

In late summer, fall, and winter, *Calamagrostis* x *acutiflora* 'Overdam' (feather reed grass) is an exquisite grass specimen. A colleague, aware of my love for grasses, gave me a start of this plant during one of my rendezvous at the Denver Botanic Gardens. When I first had the small specimen, I tried to imagine where this grass might look its best. I placed it near a path and at the bottom of a small hill, so visitors could touch and admire it. Though it spreads to only about eighteen inches, it grows almost four feet high in my garden, exhibiting smooth, compressed, variegated white-and-green foliage. Its linear leaves, along with a golden inflorescence, make it an ideal mate for *Rosa* 'Golden Wings', which is planted a foot away. The growth habit of this rose is open and slightly spreading. The older stems are thorny, thick, and brown; newer growth is less prickly, with twisted red and green branches veering off to each side. When it blooms, the dark orange, yellow-eyed flower harmonizes beautifully with the golden color of 'Overdam'.

Panicums with Panache

A discussion of ornamental grasses for fall and winter would be incomplete without delving into the many types of *Panicum* (switch grass). The nearly five hundred annual and perennial species are native to the deserts, forests, swamps, and temperate zones of North America. After being ignored for decades, panicums are finally being appreciated for their enormous decorative contribution to the home landscape. They are a diverse group of plants, varying in height from approximately four to eight feet. Culture is easy. Once established, most are drought tolerant and will work well in clay or sandy soils. Self-sowing is usually minimal, but may be prolific if soil is continually moist. Except for the annual practice of

Texture and contrast are abundant here as the Iris leaves and flowers play off the wrought iron bench.
The face of the stone cat pokes though *Sedum globosum* 'Old Man's Bones'
as the greenery of rose 'Hiawatha' snakes its way among the flowers.

shearing them back to a few inches in early spring, these upright grasses, like most others, are practically maintenance free. If supplementary water is needed (which it seldom is), the leaves will curl, sending out a signal to the gardener. These grasses offer a broad range of showy colors and profusely branched inflorescences that are finely textured. Summer leaf color can be shades of powdery blue to deep green and, in fall, a spectrum of tones appear, featuring yellows, wine-reds, and varying nuances of beige. The panicums bloom in July and August, and the inflorescences are usually tinted pink or red when they first open.

For many years I have been pleased with the effect of *Panicum virgatum* 'Heavy Metal'. Its metallic blue leaves stand stiff and upright, like soldiers dressed to the nines standing guard at a palace. In autumn the leaves turn yellow. The extremely delicate flowers, which resemble tiny teardrops, reliably last into winter. I have placed this grass near various sedums, penstemons, and euphorbias—perennials that, with their patchwork of dissimilar colors and lines, create a pleasant jumbling effect opposed to the dainty grass.

A new panicum, which I have grown for just a short while, is *P. virgatum* 'Dallas Blues'. The blue foliage, which in fall slowly dries to beige tinted burnt orange, is three-quarters of an inch wide, wider than that of most other panicums. It grows to five feet and may eventually reach that width as well. I'll watch as it matures in the coming years because I'm curious to see how statuesque and blue the plumes will be. The few that I have seen are a foot long, and have the extravagant appearance of a swishing horse's tail. Because of its dynamic color, I predict it will be a hot seller at nurseries in future years.

Another selection that I recently planted is *P. virgatum* 'Cloud Nine', which has glaucous foliage and foot-long golden inflorescences atop stems that will reach about five feet in the Intermountain West, with vivid fall coloration. I have planted this one in the middle of a border primarily composed of shrubs, whose larger leaves of various shapes create a nice contrast in form.

Microclimates

My property is in USDA zone 5, meaning, in general, plants can withstand low temperatures to minus twenty degrees F. Still, I sometimes experiment and buy plants if they are designated zone 6 or warmer. Zone maps are rough guides that help, to some extent, to predict what will work in each region. *Miscanthus sinensis* 'Yaku Jima' falls into this category, as do many of my other grasses and perennials. To help the more temperamental or less hardy plants, I will mulch them, put them in a protected spot, or just hope that the winter will be mild—which has been the case for the past six or so years.

Microclimates—small areas where variations in temperature and exposure occur, caused by the interactions of air, water, sun, soil, and other vegetation—are found naturally in any garden, providing niches or somewhat sheltered spots. I make good use of mine. Years ago I remember reading a famous garden author who stated that *Zauschneria californica* (hummingbird trumpet) was hardy only to zone 8. But I, and other Western gardeners, have tried it and found it to be quite hardy and adaptable to our region. My zauschneria is planted next to a rock with which it bonds and which keeps it warmer in winter by absorbing heat and providing shelter from winds. My backyard, without many large trees, often has strong winds rushing through it. Boulders of various sizes, strategically placed, give protection to some of my plants. But even in more exposed sites *Z. californica* has survived well for many gardeners in cold climates. I take chances with plants and stretch the zones. I do keep some sanity with this experiment, realizing that a palm tree won't grow in my climate, or at least not outdoors in the winter. Neither will the more tender annual grass *Pennisetum setaceum* 'Rubrum' (purple-leaved fountain grass), but I like this grass, topped with graceful burgundy plumes, so I use it in areas where I want the lines of grasses and reddish color for one season and am willing to replace it for the next.

Some gardeners play it safe and purchase only plants that are supposed to fit in their particular zone. I like taking risks and experimenting with some plants. If they are irresistible, I'll buy them and see whether they will adapt to my garden. I have seen good results with such experiments in my region, especially with certain so-called annual grasses such as *Cortaderia selloana* 'Andes Silver' and 'Patagonia' (pampas grass). The Denver Botanic Gardens has planted sweeps of these two varieties in a meadowy setting, where they look spectacular at almost five feet high, crowned with lustrous, silvery, one-foot plumes. They have happily survived there for three years, and honestly, even if these plants do come to their demise this year or next, garden visitors still have had many opportunities to admire their foliage as they stroll through the twenty-two-acre garden.

Another zone stretcher (supposedly hardy only to zone 7, with a low of zero) I recommend for any size garden is *Stipa tenuissima* (Mexican feather grass). Rumors that this grass is an invasive pest abound. I have not had this problem in the six years I've had Mexican feather grass in my garden. Again, I think much depends on keeping it water thrifty. This clumping grass grows to about ten inches in height and has nodding, soft, almost-white stems, which are as thin as violin strings and bounce back even after they are pummeled by a few heavy snows. Concentrate a few together and you can almost hear the orchestra's violin section playing. To make good use of it, plant potent and winter-vivid groundcovers at its feet, such as sedums, thymes, and ice plants.

I encourage gardeners to be daring and see what might work under their particular and unique garden conditions. They may find it exciting to play with the elements, such as rain, snow, and rocks, and be delightfully surprised about unforeseen successes. Experimentation brings adventure into the plant world and to our doorsteps.

Silver, Sedums, and Stone

Shades of silver are special in the garden when they aren't overused. Whether you use silvery annuals such as *Senecio* (dusty miller) that can be perennial depending on the severity of your winter, or silvery perennials such as *Santolina chamaecyparissus* (lavender cotton), these powerful accents add a sparkle to practically any landscape with their varied textures. There are shrubby forms, as well as trees and groundcovers. I don't follow a specific technique when I use silver in my garden; rather I intuitively notice where something soft and restful is needed, or where a coarsely textured plant would stimulate the setting. Other times, I totally bow to the art of improvisation, and put the plant in an empty area (if I can find one) and work other plants with color artistically around it.

In fall I enjoy the reflection of the sun as it appears to fade and glow, accentuating plants and garden structures alike. Practically any kind of stone, when linked with silver-leafed plants, enhances the total picture. Silver seems to awaken the garden. Toward the back end of one of my garden beds a wall of maroon rocks, touched with green lichen, trails off toward my property fence line. On top of this wall are planted a few clumps of *Artemisia stelleriana* 'Silver Brocade'. Here it receives scarcely any moisture from the hose, getting a sprinkling only now and then because the spot is hard to reach, yet it thrives. Too much water and it would certainly rot. The light gray, chrysanthemum-like leaves of the artemisia tightly hug the smooth surface of the stone, sliding into a few openings that are just begging to be filled. With imagination, low sedums could be added to this exhibit to complement the silver plant and the sturdy rocks.

Thanks to my daughter-in-law, I am now aware of another use for *Seriphidium canum* (silver sagebrush). When my son Gabe and his wife Gloria were married, the late-August celebration took place in my garden. Gloria wanted some kind of "crown" to commemorate her marriage. Using dried rose petals, grasses, herbs, sagebrush, and distinctive seedheads, she wove a Grecian crown, which I keep as a memento. For a moment, when I glanced at her, I felt catapulted back to a time when Roman gladiators, kings, and queens were all brought together for a feast. Gloria made another excellent use of sagebrush when she cut a few stems into long narrow strips. A friend brought over some red embroidery thread, which Gloria twisted in a circular fashion around each three-inch strip of sage that was well covered with leaves. Before leaving the celebration, each guest was given one of these silver-and-red scented souvenirs.

Aside from the pungent aroma and the silver accent of *Seriphidium canum*, it has many medicinal and practical uses. *A. absinthium* (common wormwood) is recognized as an effective insect repellent. It is used in sachets to keep moths away and is planted in gardens to discourage pests such as black flea beetles and slugs. (Thankfully, those pests don't travel in my neighborhood.) Tea made of it and sprayed on plants will repel aphids. (In spring, when aphids blacken my *Seriphidium canum*, I need only wait a week or two and petite ladybugs come along and gobble up the aphids!)

A silver plant that blends beautifully with a variety of sedums is *Anthemis marschalliana* subsp. *biebersteiniana*, formerly *Anthemis biebersteinii* or *A. biebersteiniana* (filigree daisy), a fanciful, ornamental work of art that forms a cushiony mound up to a foot across. This spring-blooming jewel has small yellow daisies atop six- to ten-inch stems. Group a few together, accent them with sedum, and you have orchestrated a visually graphic scenario. *A. marschalliana* subsp. *biebersteiniana*, like most silvery plants, needs to be kept on the dry side with good drainage; otherwise, it will simply die. I know this from personal experience, since I made the mistake of overwatering it in another section of my garden and lost it very quickly.

Certain varieties of artemisia are aggressive. Many gardeners have banned *A. ludoviciana* (white sage, sometimes known as wormwood) from their gardens because of its vigorous

Artemesia ludoviciana 'Valerie Finnis' cascades over garden stone.

growth habit. Its natural and rugged habitat is large, ranging from the prairies of Nebraska to the foothills of the Rockies. In these areas soils are mostly dry, lean (some sandy, others are dense and claylike), and rocky. The gray-green, dissected, medium-size leaves are downy, and the plant generally grows two to four feet. It looks lovely and simple growing naturally among boulders, yellow daisies, and other wild plants, where no one is shoveling in compost or constantly bathing it with water.

Some gardeners have also stopped planting *Artemisia ludoviciana* 'Valerie Finnis', with its soft, feltlike, gray, two-inch leaves. It can definitely spread, but being stingy with water and not amending its soil curtails some of its characteristic invasiveness. Another method of limiting its friendly nature is to give portions of it away. When I give plants to neighbors, I explain the plant's needs, telling them the pluses and minuses, then allowing them to make the final decision. Even those neighbors who are not gardeners may appreciate the plant if they have a particular niche that needs to be filled. For instance, they may have a spot in a part of their garden that hoses can't reach, yet they do not want the area to be weedy and they are not into planting shrubs or trees. This sage would be ideal; it would add a touch of silver, spread quickly, and hold down weeds.

I like this plant. I also like knowing that there really is a Valerie Finnis. She is an aristocrat (Lady Scot) from England, who at this writing is secretary of the Merlin Trust, an organization in England that funds future horticulturists. Ms. Finnis passed a piece of this plant on to Beth Chatto, the English gardener well known for her fabulous and always expanding gardens in East Anglia. This region is one of the driest areas in England, with an annual rainfall of eighteen inches (as compared to thirty inches or more for most portions of Great Britain), so in Beth Chatto's garden 'Valerie Finnis' stays more compact.

In any spot where I am careful not to overwater, I unite artemisias with sedums. The silver of artemisia foliage and the varying tints of the sedums make great companions. For example, in a sunny dry section, I planted an unknown, small-leafed red sedum, probably obtained when I volunteered at the Denver Botanic Gardens. It has diminutive, red crinkled leaves and creeps over a low wall made out of old granite hunks that are full of sparkly bits. Above the wall, the gray leaves of *Artemisia* 'Valerie Finnis' tumble over the edge, mingling with the sedum and stone. The hard-surfaced granite wall is both background player and unifying element as these plants bake and bask with abandon under the hot sun.

The colors of sedums intensify during fall and winter. Their fleshy, succulent stems, which speak to their drought tolerance, come in varying shades of greens, grays, and reds, with rosettes that are amusing and complex. In most cases, these are easy-care plants that like full sun and good drainage. Heights range from a few inches to over two feet. A choice low grower is *S. spathulifolium* 'Carnea', whose frosted greenery is highlighted with crimson. 'Carnea' is decked in summer with tiny yellow flowers. Sedum 'Autumn Joy' grows over two feet tall and produces large, flat clusters of red or pink florets that bloom in August/September against gray-green foliage.

One sedum that gets my undivided attention is *S.* 'Mohrchen', which was given to me by a colleague when I admired it in her garden. It sits melodramatically at the bottom of a berm near a path that I frequent and has grown about two feet high. With pink flowers and brick-red leaves flecked green, it flaunts itself against a massive, smooth stone, with the light blue flowers of *Salvia azurea* (pitcher sage) in the background. I also like 'Mohrchen' because the stems vary in height and bend a bit, so that some are shorter and others slightly taller, adding a touch of the exotic to the picture. They remind me of organ pipes of varying heights that make different musical sounds.

Sedums are also appropriate in both mixed and perennial borders. I impulsively place them wherever I want to add spark to a fall scene. Three recent introductions to try are *S. telephium* 'Matrona', *S.* 'Neon', and a variegated variety called *S. alboroseum* 'Frosty Morn'. From my viewpoint, 'Matrona' rivals the overfamiliar *S.* 'Autumn Joy'. Like 'Autumn Joy', it will grow to two feet in height, but its gray-green succulent leaves are etched in burgundy, and the flowers at the top are soft red, demanding attention when blended with yellow sunflowers and rudbeckias. As its popularity grows, I believe this new sedum will become a hit among seasoned flower lovers who, perhaps like me, have become bored with 'Autumn Joy.'

The second new variety, *S.* 'Neon,' grows under a foot tall and shouts out like a neon sign flashing for attention along the highway. The flowers are purple-pink; its wide leaves are light green. I imagine that 'Neon' would fit perfectly in front of a rock wall, bursting with its richly colored flowers; it also adds variety and fall color placed anywhere in a small perennial border, which is where I recently planted two of them.

S. alboroseum was brought to this country from Japan by plant collector and nurseryman Barry Yinger. It grows about a foot tall, and the fall flowers look like little stars of pale pink and white. The highlight of this sedum are its leaves, which are etched in white.

Traveling along a short wall in my garden near 'Valerie Finnis' is the mound-forming *Sedum globosum* (Old Man's Bones). I came across this sedum accidentally when I was at a nursery looking at garden tools one year around Thanksgiving. Since it was late in the season, many plants were half price, and I was forced to wander the plant department and take a peek! (I can't resist a sale, especially if there is something I don't have.) With such an out-of-the-ordinary name, and with its cute appearance, I instinctively bought it and tucked it in around a few rocks. This low sedum has many small, mid-green, globular puffed leaves attached, in segments, to its red-tinged stem. I like how it snuggles near the gray leaves of 'Valerie Finnis', and I'm pleased that I trusted my internal hunch to buy it.

On the south side of my property, where it stays hot and dry, I again trusted my instincts and brought together a few special plants. I used *Sedum reflexum* 'Blue Spruce' and *S.* 'Vera Jameson'. 'Blue Spruce' is very low and has a blue cast to it, a nice choice for a rockery. Let it meander wherever it chooses. I have it in front of *S.* 'Vera Jameson', a stonecrop with reddish, gray and blue sprawling foliage that remains under a foot tall and has light pink flowers on top. Instinctively I placed the broad, ten-inch-high *Artemisia versicolor* 'Sea Foam' (curlicue sage) nearby, where it shoots a puff of silver into the panorama. This sage grows to five feet across and is one of my newly favorite silver plants, whose strength lies in its opulence. Use this plant in a level area of your garden, as I have done, or experiment and let it curl over any kind of rock wall. In autumn, if snow has not settled in, the entire plant is accented with pink highlights. Also included in this plant entourage is the East Coast native *Eriogonum allenii* (buckwheat). It blooms for a long time in fall with chartreuse-and-red-tinted bracts and bold, floppy, green-red leaves. Even though it's from the East, I find it does well with minimal water and a gravelly soil mix. It's an eriogonum quite unlike most others, whose umbel flowers are usually frothy or whose habit is small and low. This one forms a mat, but the leaves are four inches long and two inches wide. Above them, to two feet, rise fine-textured branches topped by large umbels. This plant may be difficult to find locally or in catalogs. Perhaps in the future, nurseries will try to propagate it.

Another excellent silver foliage plant for dry areas is *A. ludoviciana* 'Silver Frost'. It grows to about fifteen inches with a spread of three feet. A nice combination will result if, as I have done, you surround it with dark-colored *Sempervirens*.

A plant that I welcomed into my garden a few years ago is a shrubby *Helichrysum* (strawflower). Helichrysums mostly hail from Europe, Australia, and Western Asia. This one, *Helichrysum splendidum* (syn. *H. trilineatum*), is from South Africa, and it has made a cozy home in my rock garden. When I first planted it, the shrub performed poorly; it also looked as though some creature had snatched a bite from its side. I couldn't figure out what in the world was damaging the plant. Last year a raccoon snuck in the cat door and nibbled at fruit on my kitchen table. I was asleep when this invasion happened. To my relief he left quietly and quickly, before more damage was done! Perhaps he had also sampled the strawflower? I finally discovered that each time I watered, the spray from the hose shot out too strongly, eventually injuring the stems. Once I changed that practice the helichrysum recovered substantially, gradually putting on new growth and blooming successfully. It is a bushy, globe-shaped shrub with ivory stems and a silvery gleam to it. For me it grows about eighteen inches high and spreads to two feet. In summer the clustered flowerheads are sunshine yellow, and through most falls the foliage remains a silvery light green. Even as the ample golden flower color fades, dainty seed capsules, appearing like drooping tassels, remain pale yellow. This coloring continues even as winter coats the landscape.

Many of the helichrysums, because of the nature of their flowers, which are very papery and appear to be dry even when fresh, are excellent candidates for dried arrangements. I visualize a few of these flowers in a small vase on the breakfast table on a cold winter's day. For best appearance, after a few years, it's a good idea to prune this plant down to five or six inches in early spring. This practice will keep it from becoming leggy with age and will maintain its tight form.

At the base of this plant and for terrific textural accent I have placed *Picea pungens* 'Glauca Procumbens' (trailing blue spruce). The long, curving, blue-gray stems of this spruce poke into the helichrysum to create the kind of foliage duo that passionate gardeners adore! To pep up such a scene, scatter different forms of sedums around these plants. I am particularly fond of *Sedum spathulifolium* 'Cape Blanco', and I like it nudged up to this pair. This sedum forms a carpet of blue tones in summer and turns gray in fall and winter. Its shades, mixed in with the pearly stems and yellow fading flowers of the helichrysum, bring diversity to a little-watered section of the garden.

In recent years, *Artemisia* 'Powis Castle' has become popular because of its billowing habit, filigree foliage, and elegant appearance. It is an excellent plant for dotting around the landscape, which is exactly what I have done. Given adequate space and good drainage, it has spread to five feet in my garden and reaches a height of two feet. With too much water the inner stems become brown and look shabby and the normal cloudy form of the plant becomes tacky and leggy. However, other gardeners in my region have had success with it, even when it has been given additional water. So experiment and see if it will work for you.

Companion plants for this artemisia are easy to find. Along with sedums and plants with pastel flowers, I have used *Salvia officinalis* 'Tricolor' (tricolor sage) and *S. azurea* (pitcher sage). The first has scented variegated leaves of cream, pink, and green and plays off the foliage of *Artemisia* 'Powis Castle'. At a height of four feet, *S. azurea* displays whorls of many clear blue, three-quarter-inch flowers on long spikes. It acts as a great background plant in many garden situations because of its stately demeanor. If you are lucky and can keep moisture at bay, *S. azurea* will pop up in other low-water areas of your garden, adding the blue color gardeners crave in the autumn landscape. Let the reseeding annual cosmos *C. bipinnatus* pop up around any mass of gray plants. One final suggestion for use with this silvery artemisia is the annual grass *Pennisetum setaceum* 'Rubrum', noted for its burgundy foliage and plumes.

For a dry site, or perhaps a small rock garden, I cherish *Artemisia pycnocephala* 'David's Choice'. It forms a low cushion, only about five inches high, and can spread almost a foot. It is silkily tomentose (meaning that it is closely covered with fine hairs), and as I walk through my garden I cup my palm and give it a gentle pat, taking pleasure in its smoothness and its compact form.

For another sparkling combination with grays, try *Dianthus nardiformis* (cloud pink), one of the few pinks that bloom in late summer and into fall with profuse lavender color. As part

Picea pungens 'Globosa' (spruce) and *Tulipa batalinii* 'Bright Gem'
complement each other well.

of this picture, the thin, tubular orange flowers of *Zauschneria californica* will add punch and rivet the attention of gardeners and non-gardeners alike.

With silver plants, attractive seedheads, and more, fall and winter are rich in color and form. Plants go dormant during this quiet time, but I am still drawn to the texture of grasses and to small, luscious red rose hips as they dangle and wait patiently for the seasons to transform.

As winter approaches and settles in, I take pleasure in seeing waves of snow blanket different sections of the garden. On days when the sweetness of the sun shines and melts the snow, I admire the low cushions of sunroses as they hug the pebbly pea gravel, dressed in their grayish green foliage. Although I relish this restful time of year, I greatly anticipate the day when the sunroses will be smothered with tiny buds that will burst open in the spring sunshine.

Acknowledgments

The technicalities of writing a book are more complex than I ever dreamed of. Friends and colleagues helped me along this journey. In regard to research and horticultural information, former Denver Botanic Gardens librarian Susan Eubank was very helpful and always there to assist me, as was expert horticulturist Kelly Grummons, who also read my manuscript.

For his friendship, horticultural wisdom, and generosity with plants and time, I am grateful to Panayoti Kelaidis, Curator of Plant Collections at Denver Botanic Gardens. He opened up doors for me that I never knew existed. Lauren Springer unknowingly inspired me with her books.

As I began unraveling the complexity of roses, Bill Campbell and Marlea Graham graciously read portions of my rose chapter. Regarding shrub roses grown locally, Marilyn Wells kindly opened up her garden. When I had questions concerning certain plants, Mary Ellen Tonsing, Rebecca Day-Skowron, Harriet McMillian, and Gwen Kelaidis willingly shared their knowledge.

Kay Galvan, Jane Shellenberger, and Marie Morrison assisted me with critical feedback about my manuscript. I especially appreciated the editing help and advice of Leslie Heizer. Upon acceptance of my manuscript, Marlene Blessing, like a conductor at a symphony, cheered on my voice.

Bibliography and Selected Readings

Agriculture and Agri-Food Canada Publication 1922/E. *Winter Hardy Roses*. Ottawa: Minister of Public Works and Government Services Canada, 1996.

Armitage, Allan M. *Armitage's Garden Perennials*. Portland, OR: Timber Press, 2000.

Austin, David. *David Austin's English Roses*. New York: Little, Brown and Co., 1993.

Bailey, Liberty Hyde, and Ethel Zoe Bailey, revised and expanded by the staff of Liberty Hyde Bailey Hortorium. *Hortus Third: A Concise Dictionary of Plants Cultivated in the United States and Canada*. New York: Macmillan, 1976.

Bärtels, Andreas, translated by Roberta J. Cooper. *Gardening with Dwarf Trees and Shrubs*. Portland, OR: Timber Press, 1986.

Bath, Trevor, and Joy Jones. *The Gardener's Guide to Growing Hardy Geraniums*. Portland, OR: Timber Press, 1994.

Beales, Peter. *Roses*. New York: Henry Holt and Co., 1992.

Beckett, Kenneth, ed. *Encyclopedia of Alpines*, Vol. 1. Pershore, Worcestershire [England]: AGS Publications Ltd., 1993.

————. *Encyclopedia of Alpines*, Vol. 2. Pershore, Worcestershire [England]: AGS Publications Ltd., 1994.

Betts, Edwin M., and Hazlehurst Bolton Perkins. *Thomas Jefferson's Flower Garden at Monticello*. Charlottesville: University Press of Virginia, 1986.

Brickell, Christopher, and David Joyce. *The American Horticultural Society Pruning and Training*. New York: DK Publishing, Inc., 1996.

Charlesworth, Geoffrey. *A Gardener Obsessed*. Boston: David R. Godine, 1994.

Chatto, Beth. *Beth Chatto's Gravel Garden*. New York: Viking Studio, 2000.

Clausen, Ruth Rogers, and Nicholas H. Ekstrom. *Perennials for American Gardens*. New York: Random House, 1989.

Cuthbertson, Yvonne. *Women Gardeners*. Denver, CO: Arden Press, 1998.

Darke, Rick. *The Color Encyclopedia of Ornamental Grasses*. London: The Orion Publishing Group, 1999.

Darke, Rick (consulting ed.) and Mark Griffiths (series ed.). *Manual of Grasses*. Portland, OR: Timber Press, 1994.

Davies, Dilys. *Allium, The Ornamental Onion*. Portland, OR: Timber Press, 1989.

Denver Water. *Xeriscape Plant Guide*. Golden, CO: Fulcrum Publishing, 1996.

Dickerson, Brent C. *The Old Rose Adventurer*. Portland, OR: Timber Press, 1999.

Dirr, Michael A. *Dirr's Hardy Trees and Shrubs*. Portland, OR: Timber Press, 2000.

————. *Manual of Woody Landscape Plants: Their Identification, Ornamental Characteristics, Culture, Propagation, and Uses*. Champaign, IL: Stripes Publishing Co., 1990.

Eck, Joseph. *Elements of Garden Design*. New York: Henry Holt and Co., 1996.

Elliott, Clarence. *Rock Garden Plants*. London: E. Arnold & Co., 1935.

Fingerut, Joyce, and Rex Murfitt. *Creating and Planting Garden Troughs*. Wayne, PA: B. B. Mackey Books, 1999.

Foster, H. Lincoln. *Rock Gardening*. Portland, OR: Timber Press, 1968 (1982).

Glattstein, Judy. *The American Gardener's World of Bulbs*. New York: Little, Brown and Co., 1994.

Graham, Marlea. "The Hundred Years' War: Own-root vs. Budded Roses." *American Rose Annual* (1994), vol. XXI no. 24, pp. 66–70.

Greenlee, John. *The Encyclopedia of Ornamental Grasses*. Emmaus, PA: Rodale Press, 1992.

Grey-Wilson, Christopher. *Poppies.* Portland, OR: Timber Press, 1993.

Griffiths, Mark. *Index of Garden Plants.* Portland, OR: Timber Press, 1995.

Hansen, Richard, and Friedrich Stahl. *Perennials and Their Garden Habitats.* Portland, OR: Timber Press, 1993.

Hylton, William, and Claire Kowalchik, eds. *Rodale's Illustrated Encyclopedia of Herbs.* Emmaus, PA: Rodale Press, 1987.

Knopf, Jim. *The Xeriscape Flower Gardener.* Boulder, CO: Johnson Books, 1991.

Loewer, Peter. *The Annual Garden.* Emmaus, PA: Rodale Press, 1988.

Martin, Laura C. *Garden Flower Folklore.* Chester, CT: The Globe Pequot Press, 1987.

McGourty, Frederick. *The Perennial Gardener.* Boston: Houghton, Mifflin Co., 1989.

McKeon, Judith C. *The Encyclopedia of Roses.* Emmaus, PA: Rodale Press, 1995.

Neal, Bill. *Gardener's Latin.* Chapel Hill, NC: Algonquin Books of Chapel Hill, 1992.

Newton, James. *Uncommon Friends: Life with Thomas Edison, Henry Ford, Harvey Firestone, Alexis Carrel and Charles Lindbergh.* San Diego, CA: Harcourt, Brace, Jovanovich, 1987.

Nold, Robert. *Penstemons.* Portland, OR: Timber Press, 1999.

Olds, Margaret, ed. *Botanica's Roses.* New York: Mynah, 1998.

Osborne, Robert. *Hardy Roses.* Pownal, VT: Storey Communications, Inc., 1991.

Ottesen, Carole. *Ornamental Grasses: The Amber Wave.* San Francisco: McGraw-Hill Publishing Co., 1989.

Pesman, M. Walter. *Meet the Natives.* Denver, CO: Robert Rinehart Publishers, 1992.

Phillips, Roger, and Martyn Rix. *The Quest for the Rose.* New York: Random House, 1993.

Proctor, Rob. *Naturalizing Bulbs.* New York: Henry Holt and Co., Inc., 1997.

Reilly, Ann. *The Rose.* New York: Portland House, 1989.

Robinson, William. *The English Flower Garden.* 1889. Reprint, New York: Amaryllis Press, 1984.

———. *The Wild Garden.* 1895. Reprint, Portland, OR: Timber Press, 1994.

Seabrook, Peter. "Am I a Latin Lover?" *Journal of the Royal Horticultural Society, The Garden,* Vol. 125, Part 7 (July 2000), pp. 556–58.

Silk, Steve. "Stone Adds Naturalistic Structure to Any Garden." *Fine Gardening,* # 76 (Dec. 2000), pp. 14 and 16.

Springer, Lauren. *The Undaunted Garden.* Golden, CO: Fulcrum Publishing, 1994.

Springer, Lauren, and Rob Proctor. *Passionate Gardening.* Golden, CO: Fulcrum Publishing, 2000.

Tatroe, Marcia. *Perennials for Dummies.* Foster City, CA: IDG Books Worldwide, Inc., 1997.

Thomas, Graham Stuart. *Ornamental Shrubs, Climbers and Bamboos.* Portland, OR: Timber Press, 1992.

———. *The Rock Garden and Its Plants: From Grotto to Alpine House.* Portland, OR: Timber Press, 1989.

———. *Perennial Garden Plants.* Portland, OR: Timber Press. 1990.

———. *The Graham Stuart Thomas Rose Book.* Portland, OR: Timber Press, 1994.

Turner, Roger. *Euphorbias.* Portland, OR: Timber Press, 1995.

Verrier, Suzanne. *Rosa Gallica.* Deer Park, WI: Capability's Books, 1995.

Verrier, Suzanne. *Rosa Rugosa.* Deer Park, WI: Capability's Books, 1991.

Wilder, Louise Beebe. *The Rock Garden.* Garden City, NY: Doubleday, Doran & Co., 1933.

Williams, Jean, ed. *Rocky Mountain Alpines.* Portland, OR: Timber Press, 1996.

Winterrowd, Wayne. *Annuals for Connoisseurs.* New York: Prentice-Hall, Inc., 1992.

Zuzek, Kathy, Marcia Richards, Steve McNamara, and Harold Pellett. *Roses for the North.* Minnesota Report 237-1995. St. Paul, Minnesota : Minnesota Agricultural Experiment Station, University of Minnesota.

Select Mail-Order Rose Catalogs, Plus Sources for Perennials and Grasses

THE ANTIQUE ROSE EMPORIUM
9300 Lueckemeyer Road
Brenham, TX 77833-6453
Phone: 979-441-0002
Fax: 979-836-0928
Website: www.weAREroses.com
Large selection; good reference guide.

CORN HILL NURSERY, LTD.
Rural Route 5
Petitcodiac, New Brunswick EOA 2HO
CANADA
Phone: 506-756-3635
Fax: 506-756-1087
Specializes in hardy roses. Mostly own-root; shipping bareroot April 15 to May 15.

FORESTFARM
990 Tetherow Road
Williams, OR 97544-9599
Phone: 541-846-7269
Website: www.forestfarm.com
Good selection of species and own-root shrubs. Well-stocked in perennials.

HEIRLOOM OLD GARDEN ROSES
24062 NE Riverside Drive
St. Paul, OR 97137
Phone: 503-538-1576
Website: www.heirloomroses.com
Good selection of Old Garden roses, shrub roses, David Austin roses, and more. All grown own-root.

HERONSWOOD NURSERY, LTD.
7530 NE 288th Street
Kingston, WA 98346-9502
Phone: 360-297-4772
Website: www.heronswood.com
Species roses and a large and unusual selection of perennials.

HIGH COUNTRY GARDENS
2902 Rufina Street
Santa Fe, NM 87507-2929
Phone: 1-800-925-9387
Website: www.highcountrygardens.com
Excellent selection of xeriscape plants, ornamental grasses, and cold-hardy shrub roses.

HIGH COUNTRY ROSES
P.O. Box 148
Jensen, UT 84035
Phone: 435-789-5512 / 800 552-2082
Good selection.

KURT BLUEMEL, INC.
2740 Green Lane
Baldwin, MD 21013-9523
Phone: 1-800-498-1560
Website: www.bluemel.com
Famous for ornamental grasses. Carries perennials also.

LOWE'S OWN-ROOT ROSES
6 Sheffield Road
Nashua, NH 03062
Phone: 603-888-2214
Unusual species and Old Garden roses. Good selection; must order eighteen months ahead.

PICKERING NURSERIES, INC.
670 Kingston Road
Pickering, Ontario L 1V 1A6
CANADA
Website: www.pickeringnurseries.com

PLANTS OF THE SOUTHWEST
3095 Aqua Fria
Santa Fe, NM 87507
Phone: 1-800-788-7333
Website: www.plantsofthesouthwest.com
Mail-order plants only through the end of 2002. Excellent choices for dryland perennials and grasses.

PRAIRIE NURSERY
P.O. Box 306
Westfield, WI 53964
Phone: 1-800-476-9453
Website: www.prairienursery.com
Wide selection of native prairie grasses as well as perennials for dry and moist climates.

ROSES UNLIMITED
Route 1, Box 587
Laurens, SC 29360
Phone: 864-682-7673
Website: www.rosesunlimitedownroot.com

ROSLYN NURSERY
211 Burrs Lane
Dix Hills, NY 11746
Phone: 631-643-9347
Website: www.roslynnursery.com
Specializes in shade-tolerant perennials, grasses, and vines.

SAM KEDEM NURSERY AND GARDEN
12414 191st Street
Hastings, MT 55033
Phone: 651-437-7516
Fax: 651-437-7195
Email: theKedems@aol.com

VINTAGE GARDENS
2833 Old Gravenstein Highway South
Sebastopol, CA 95472
Phone: 707-829-2035
Website: www.vintagegardens.com
Large selection; excellent and thorough descriptions.

Index

(Pages in boldface indicate photographs.)